Listen to the Children
From Focused Observation to Strategic Instruction

Jane Fraser

Heinemann
Portsmouth, NH

Heinemann
A division of Reed Elsevier Inc.
361 Hanover Street
Portsmouth, NH 03801-3912
www.heinemann.com

Offices and agents throughout the world

The author and publisher wish to thank those who granted permission to reprint borrowed material:

Excerpts from *Time to Teach, Time to Learn: Changing the Pace of School* by Chip Wood. Copyright © 1999. Published by Northeast Foundation for Children, Greenfield, Massachusetts. Reprinted by permission of the publisher.

Library of Congress Cataloging-in-Publication Data

Fraser, Jane.
    Listen to the children : from focused observation to strategic instruction / Jane Fraser.
       p. cm.
    Includes bibliographical references and index.
    ISBN 0-325-00403-X (alk. paper)
    1. Observation (Educational method).   2. Elementary school teaching.
  I. Title.

LB1027.28 .F75 2002
372.1102—dc21   2002024225

Editor: Lois Bridges
Production coordinator: Sonja S. Chapman
Production service: Colophon
Cover design: Jenny Jensen Greenleaf
Author photo: Sarah Merriman Spencer
Typesetter: G & S Typesetters
Manufacturing: Steve Bernier

Printed in the United States of America on acid-free paper
06 05 04 03 02 RRD 1 2 3 4 5

To my teachers: Anna, Anthony, Brian, Caila, Chester, Dan, Dylan, Franci, Gabriele, Josh, Kate, Logan, Mark, Melissa, Natasha, and Paige

Contents

Acknowledgments

These pages could not have been written without the generous assistance of many skillful teachers, though the central idea, listening to children, was generated by the comment of a second-grade student. These teachers invited me into their classrooms for regular observations over an extended time.

Here you will meet Julianne Dow, Karen Wrobel Feiss, Whitney McCarthy, Nancy Kovacic, Kate Miserocchi, Stephanie Schock, Mara Schwartz, and Sarah Merriman Spencer at Coleytown Elementary School in Westport, Connecticut, and visit with their students. You will also meet Deb Bell and Nicole Fieschel and their students at Greens Farms School in Westport, and Beth Eccleston plus her class in New Rochelle, New York. I spent most of my research time in the classrooms of Whitney, Mara, Kate, and Sarah, scripting minilessons, class discussions, and informal conversations. I visited these rooms on a regular, weekly schedule during one school year.

I want to thank Caltha Crowe, Curriculum Resource Teacher in Westport, for her friendship and specific help with details about curriculum and expectations at Coleytown Elementary School. I am indebted to Donna Skolnick, writing companion and special friend, who will read my words and share her unique thinking whenever I ask. An extra mention of Sarah Merriman Spencer is in order. She was the teacher who generously spent so much time helping me process observations to understand the possible impact of this project. And, thanks to Kaye May, Principal at Coleytown Elementary School.

Kudos to Lois Bridges, for I cannot imagine a more willing and ready editor. She would not say, but I will: her delicate and kindly fingerprints are in many places here, and I am grateful that she is such a skilled professional and fine friend. I also need to say how grateful I am to my husband, Julius, for his unconditional and loving support. This has been a long and joyful journey, one on which I received assistance from many special people in my life.

User's Guide

Dear Reader,

While I wish I could visit in your classroom or meet with you to talk about teaching, let's do the next best thing. Through the pages of this book, we can visit some incredible classrooms to meet the teachers, to watch and listen as they interact with their students. Our visits will spark introspection as they invite you to reflect on your own teaching as well as your ways of living and learning with your students.

What's written inside these covers is intended to be practical. It is divided into stories or vignettes, each of which can be read separately. These accounts do not have to be read in the order in which they appear, but can be used in any sequence. In other words, begin where it seems most relevant to your current work.

I do suggest that you start with the first section, "Observation and Reflection: Put Power Behind Teaching and Learning." It will help you understand the rationale behind the book, which is the careful observation of students, also known as kidwatching, along with practical ways to record your observations. This section will give you pointers on how to organize your classroom for thoughtful kidwatching, and will encourage you to be reflective about the transactions among students and between yourself and students.

After you have thought about this kind of intense observation and reflection, you will be ready to read the stories in the book. Each section includes five recurring sections:

- *A reader's guide.* These are the bulleted entries just below the story title. They indicate the strategies that are discussed and explained inside the vignette, highlighting the practical ideas you can implement in your classroom.

- *Setting the scene.* Here you will discover the community, the teacher, and the grade level of the classroom in which the episode occurred.
- *The story.* This narrative—what actually happened on a particular day—will introduce you to the master teacher and the students I was observing.
- *Story background.* I have sketched in a background so you will understand the reason this vignette is important enough to look at in depth (why, for example, a teacher might plumb the depths of a snippet of recorded conversation). The story background gives you the wider context for the section you are reading. I find that new teachers, especially, are immensely grateful for this kind of information.
- *Teaching strategies.* Most important of all is the section called teaching strategies. Here you will find a variety of suggestions for teacher follow-up based upon best practices—ideas for your daily classroom life. They can be used in specific situations like those described in the story, or you can generalize them to your own personal situations. For example, consistency is a goal for every day, not only when you help a child who misplaces school materials, the focus of one story here. You will want to reach toward consistency of behavior and expectations for yourself, as the leader in the classroom, and for the students with whom you work. You will want to be continually consistent as you deal with student behavior, in how you guide children to observe the rules of the classroom, and in what you expect from children in their skill development, their homework assignments, and how they treat others. You will want to be consistent in your own behavior so students know they can count on you. The work of generalizing and transferring the suggestions about consistency is left to you, but these teaching strategies can help you find your way.

There is a glossary in the back of the book. The first time a term in the glossary appears in the text, the type will be in boldface so you can consult the glossary if it is an unfamiliar term.

The stories in this book result from my observations in grades 1 through 5. If you are teaching grade 3, for example, the practical teaching strategies that are suggested will apply to your classroom even if I have written about grade 1 or 4. You can generalize the pedagogical suggestions and transfer them into your own unique situation. Take child development into account and tailor your actions for the group with whom you are working, and modify your strategies to suit a different class next year.

The first group of stories addresses how to get along in the classroom. They are about the social and emotional concerns of students. The second group of stories describes helpful tips for organizing and managing your classroom. The last two parts contain literacy stories that target reading and writing. Many teaching strategies will work across the board and are not necessarily specific to those sections where they are discussed or the grade levels of the classrooms involved.

Review the Contents for a general idea of what you will find. Then consult the reader's guide at the beginning of each story. This guide itemizes the subsections in each vignette and provides closer direction for reading. You may wish to reconsider your practices or look for new strategies to solve a particular problem at any time during the school year. For example, if you are having problems with students understanding and following directions, you may wish to consult sections on how to clarify objectives, provide explicit teaching, give explicit instructions, and confirm understanding.

I think you will have fun reading these stories when you hear the voices of children. It is important that you enjoy being with students. Their world is unique and different from ours, with many touching and humorous surprises. If you allow yourself, you can take pleasure in stepping into their shoes for a moment to think about what they say and do. Then the serious work begins: what to do with the information you gather as you listen to children.

Most cordially,
Jane Fraser

Observation and Reflection: Put Power Behind Teaching and Learning

- **What is kidwatching?**
- **Relate kidwatching to learning**
- **Kidwatching techniques**
- **Structure the classroom environment**

At the heart of this book is our effort—as professional educators—to peer deeply into what children believe and understand. From the first day of school in August or September, teachers vigilantly ascertain the pulse of each child, to make sure each is at ease in her new school setting. This initial observation of children is soon enlarged to include each student's academic strengths and weaknesses, learning style, social adjustment, and skills. It is impossible to know what stance to take toward individual learners in the class without knowledge of each student's emotional health and skill abilities.

Jonathan Kozol (1995) writes extensively about a student named David and his struggle for learning in the poignant, heartbreaking *Amazing Grace: The Lives of Children and the Conscience of a Nation,* a book about children living in the Mott Haven section of the Bronx, New York. David, a high school student, speaks to us through the author. He informs us about his own life and belief system. Reflecting about himself, David states, "It isn't bad to sound like children. Children sometimes understand things that most grown-ups do not see" (113).

Yes, David, children have a different way of knowing. And one person who understood that was Dr. Maria Montessori, a nineteenth-century Italian physician and educator. Dr. John Lienhard (2000), of the University of Houston's College of Engineering, credits Montessori with the belief that adults have as much to learn from children as children do from adults. In this book, that premise is paramount. The book is written with the assumption that we, teachers of children, can learn a great deal from our students, and that what we learn should impact our classroom practices.

If you believe the previous sentence, you will want to tune into your students' words as they live in your classroom community. Children will show you what they have learned and what they believe with their written work and through discussion in large and small groups, formally and informally. However, you will not be able to fully process these observations unless you make some effort to document student talk and take time to reflect on it later, when you are not caught up inside the pressure cooker of daily school life.

Being an accurate, careful observer of students gives you the master key to unlock the individual door to each learner in your classroom. You will want to be prepared to act on what you see and hear once that door is wide open. Each vignette in this book takes a tiny moment of **kidwatching,** examines it, and suggests strategies that you can use in that specific situation. As well, these approaches can be generalized and transferred to other events that will occur in a myriad of ways in your classroom. You will know best how to use these strategies. I believe these stories have broad applications whether you teach in the city, the suburbs, or in a more rural school.

What Is Kidwatching?

Yetta Goodman was the first to define a teacher's act of intense observation, kidwatching. She wrote, "Teachers continuously monitor the development of their students during their daily contacts" (Goodman, Goodman and Hood 1989, 4). She continued, "Once teachers begin to take account of what they know about learning, language, and conceptual development, they then build confidence in their ability to make judgments about their students' growth. Their reflective thinking grows and takes on new dimensions" (5).

Time to reflect on classroom transactions brings the images and talk into crystal clear focus. Then it is time to consider what to do about them. Because you have a variety of pedagogical strategies in your pocket you can act and react—in other words, teach—based on these observations and your reflections on these events. Large or small moments of examination will be transformed into positive acts to facilitate meaningful student learning. You can ground much of your classroom action on Montessori's premise, learning from children. When you do that, your teaching will fit the needs of your students more precisely.

Relate Kidwatching to Learning

One of your primary jobs is to help children become literate as they live comfortably within the classroom community. Observation will help inform you where each student is in the personal learning continuum at any given time. There is not a set sequence to literacy learning or development, so kidwatching helps you understand the unique growth taking place within each student. It helps you focus your teaching on the new concepts and skills each child is ready to assimilate, whether you are instructing the whole class, small groups, or individuals. You can frame your teaching in the landscape of what students already know, which is one piece of what you can see through observation and reflection.

Kidwatching has moved into the foreground as teachers have become more firmly anchored in newer pedagogical practices. They have begun to understand how crucial it is and have learned how to make kidwatching an integral part of the day at school. Lucy Calkins (1994) says, "If we adults listen and watch closely, our children will invite us to share *their* worlds and *their* ways of living in the world. And then, when children become our teachers, showing us what they see and delight in and wonder about and reach toward, then, and only then, will we be able to extend what they know and enrich their ways of knowing" (53–54).

In *Wondrous Words: Writers and Writing in the Elementary Classroom*, Katie Wood Ray (1999) draws our attention to the link between kidwatching and assessment. She states that the "focus on information about writers is very different from the check-sheet mentality of so much traditional assessment. In the check-sheet, traditional kind of assessment, we check to make sure students *know certain things* rather than seeing *what things students know*. . . . Moving that word "know" to come after "students" actually shifts our whole paradigm from assessment that is curriculum centered to assessment that is student centered" (275). Specific examples of kidwatching and what can grow from these tiny moments of careful observation are included in the body of this book.

Kidwatching Techniques

You understand the theoretical underpinnings of why it is important to be a close observer of your students, but how can you do this in the midst of the normal hectic school day? Many teachers have developed their own systems for recording their observations. These noticings are vastly different from recording grades in a grade book. They are not only about performance. They are about questions, statements, speculations, opinions, and wonderings. Recording systems differ, but the key is a willingness to pay close attention to children throughout the school day, both during instructional moments and other, less formal times. You cannot stop kidwatching as you walk the class to physical education; something you need to know could occur right there in the hallway. In other words, as long as you are with or conferring about children, you need to be alert, with eyes and ears wide open!

It takes practice and experimentation to find a recording method that will work well for you. I recommend that you try out a variety of techniques until you are satisfied you have uncovered one with which you are comfortable. I know teachers who have decided on one system, used it for a while, and then switched to something different that would serve them better. No one system will answer all your needs—each has its strengths and weaknesses. It is like applying a coat of paint to your living room. Periodically, to keep it just right, you need to freshen or change the color. Sometimes you need a new color in short order; other times you are satisfied for the long haul.

Gather Data

I used a special notebook to do the kidwatching for this book as I scripted what was said in the classroom. At any given moment I was unsure if the talk would be meaningful, so I recorded almost everything and sifted through the pages later at home. But I was not the teacher in charge at the same time. This made the scripting very much easier. Since you will not have that luxury, do not try to record every word that is said. Instead, filter the essence of a transaction you wish to note through your mind. You can also experiment with any or several of the following methods of recording when you first begin.

- Use mailing labels attached to a clipboard that you carry around the classroom. On the top of each label, write the child's name or initials, the activity, and the date of the observation. After you write on one or more labels for a particular student, adhere the label(s) to a section of a loose-leaf notebook reserved for that child. Many teachers have found this easier than carrying a notebook around and trying to locate the right place in the notebook for each student at a given moment. (Figure 1 shows an example.)
- Use a small pack of index cards you can easily hold in your hand as you walk around the room working with individual children

10/25 JAD Writing new story @ puppy. Talked about show not tell	11/1 TTD Reading *Henry and Mudge.* Seems to enjoy. Using picture clues
10/26 JAD Continues @ pup More @ show not tell	11/1 JPP Reading *My Father's Dragon.* Seems too difficult. Monitor
JAD Tried to elicit details about pup's appearance	JPP says chose it b/c Dan is and recommended it. Check on Wed.

FIGURE 1   Mailing labels or index cards

or small groups. Again, it is helpful to write the student's name or initials plus the date and activity on the top. These cards can later be filed with others for that child in a file box or folder.

- Carry a loose-leaf notebook that is divided into sections, one for each student. Turn to the appropriate section to record an observation.
- Use a loose-leaf notebook to record the transactions among small groups of children and in the whole class during discussions and meetings. Place the date and the initials of the speaker in the margin of the paper. Using this format requires hunting through pages in the notebook when you need information on

an individual child, but you do not have to take the time to affix labels or file cards.

- Keep pre-made notebook forms on a clipboard (one page per child) for notations and plans for follow-up. When the page is full, you can file it in the notebook section for that child. (See Figure 2.)
- Use a class list that has space after each name to jot quick notes. You can reserve one sheet for reading each week and another for writing, math, social studies, or science (see Figure 3). This will not only give you a sense of what individual children say, but also help you identify who doesn't talk during group discussions or certain activities.

Name _____Jonathan_____

3/10/00 Writing—no consistent capitalization	Monitor
3/14/00 Reading—*Henry and Mudge* struggles to sound out	Talk @ other strategies, e.g., context, picture clues
3/19/00 Reading—struggling but a bit better	Teaching whole-class mini-lesson about reading strategies for unknown words

FIGURE 2   Form for notebook

Date_____ Activity_____

7

*Observation and
Reflection: Put
Power Behind
Teaching and
Learning*

Amy Bell
John Brown
Tim Cirino
Jesse Dowling
Adam French
Emily Isselin
Jamie Jackson
Carol Johnson
David King
Ann Lertman
Peter McInerny
Jonathan Nolan
Mark O'Brien
Paul Rastour
Katherine Romeo
Sarah Tarnoff
Fred Turnbull
Sam Winch

FIGURE 3   Class list

- Photocopy special sheets with a grid of boxes, one for each child. This kind of grid is especially helpful for reading and writing conferences. You can note the date and the kind of lesson you are teaching. Every box will not be filled in on a particular day, but if you use this grid for a week, you can easily see toward the end of each week which children you have overlooked. For example, if you have one sheet for writing conferences, it will help you confer with everyone. Reading conferences will be on a separate sheet. You can look through these papers quickly when collecting data for one student who you know is located in the bottom row, third column of the grid. Clipboards are wonderful for holding forms such as these. (See Figure 4.)
- Make a form that has a separate sheet for each child. One column tells the activity, the second contains your observations, and the third your interventions and/or plans. You can color code what you want to do in the future. These forms can also be kept on a clipboard. (See Figure 5.)

You may also wish to consult *Teacher to Teacher*, (Fraser 1998, 33–35), where I discuss record keeping. Personally, I find sorting through a chronological class record more time-consuming than looking through records for one student that are grouped together, but it does take extra time to put mailing labels or cards away in the appropriate place. Perhaps you can best sort and stick down mailing labels or put away index cards as you engage in the reflection piece, thus consolidating your time. You will need to go through your notations anyway as you reflect and plan. When I was thinking about minilessons, preparing to write report cards, or getting ready for parent conferences, I found the mailing labels or index cards much easier to use than a class list. I do like the grid of boxes for a different purpose—recording reading and writing conferences. So I tend to use both mailing labels and a form like Figure 4.

You may want to develop some kind of shorthand so you don't need to write out each word that is being said. For example, I write "r" for *reading* or *read;* "w" for *writing* or *write;* "2" for *to, too,* or *two;* "4" for *four* or *for;* "yr" for *your.* I often omit vowels, such as "wnt" for *went* or *want.* If there is a question later about whether I wrote *went* or *want,* the context is enough for me to recapture the actual words that were spoken. I use "&" for *and;* "@" for *at* or *about;* "b/c" for *because;* and "#" for *number.* My shorthand system speeds up and enhances accurate recording.

Date(s)_____ Activity_____

John	Jesse	Tim	Adam
Jamie	Fred	Paul	Mark
Katherine	Lauren	Will	Richard
Ann	Carol	David	Missy

FIGURE 4   Reading and writing conference notes

Name _____Emily_____

Date/Activity	Observation	Intervention/*Future Plans*
11/22 Writing Workshop	Needs to learn use of quotation marks Doesn't understand use of 's	Look at independent reading book, talked about how to determine dialogue *Do whole-class minilesson on possessives vs. plurals*
12/13 Writing Workshop	Run-on sentences	Break up into separate sentences with details about events *Monitor*
12/14 Reading	Lack of fluency	Short lesson with echo reading *Call Mom and ask her to help*
1/8	Fluency still needs work	Echo reading with Caleb and Jen *Speak with Mom again to check in and reinforce*

FIGURE 5 Individual observations plus plans

Structure the Classroom Environment

In our book *On Their Way: Celebrating Second Graders as They Read and Write* (1994), Donna Skolnick and I describe listening and talk as the power tools in the classroom. Creating a classroom where honest talk and careful listening is the currency of each day is an art; what's more, it enables accurate kidwatching. You can model and teach your students the guidelines for speaking and listening so they feel their thoughts are honored and respected. You will want to teach these guidelines aggressively and follow them consistently from the first day of school. Speaking and listening are influenced by:

- *Arranging furniture.* Desks are arranged so that everyone can easily turn to see everyone else. I prefer table groups of four desks, if possible, depending on the number of students and the size of your room. Some teachers have moved to round tables rather than desks, and students keep their supplies in special containers in the center of the tables and/or in cubbies.
- *Designating a meeting area.* Students gather in a designated **meeting area** for conversations. They are instructed ahead of time to sit in a circle or a cluster depending on the best configuration for the activity (see glossary).
- *Taking turns.* Everyone is treated with respect and is given the necessary time to finish his or her thoughts without interruption. Only one person speaks at a time, and everyone is expected to listen to the speaker.
- *Using body language.* Respectful and careful listening involves appropriate body language, including eye contact if at all possible.
- *Avoiding reverbalizing.* The person in charge does not repeat or reverbalize the words spoken by a student. This strategy encourages students to listen to each other and not be dependent on the teacher. You don't want children tuning out when peers are talking and tuning in only to you.
- *Refraining from repetitive comments.* Teach students to refrain from repetition. For example, if Jim says he likes the book because of the way the story and illustrations go together, for example, John does not repeat Jim's idea but says something different when he comments. Everyone must listen carefully in order to follow this rule.
- *Piggybacking comments.* If one student says something that sparks a thought in another child, the second student is encouraged to add onto what has been said. When using the piggyback

technique, a student gives attribution: "Karen said this book reminded her of something that happened during her soccer practice, and that reminded me of yesterday's swim team practice. Two girls got very competitive, like the characters in this book."

- *Accepting everyone's thinking.* Comments are accepted by the teacher and the students without evaluation. You can simply say "Uh huh" or acknowledge in some other way, such as shaking your head in agreement. It helps to refrain from saying "That's great" or "I agree" because this kind of evaluative comment inhibits talk. Students will worry if what they have to say is correct or important enough, and they will frame their talk for the purpose of receiving teacher approval. You can teach children to say "I have a different opinion" or other polite words when they disagree, which is certainly acceptable.

- *Allowing for wait time.* Model **wait time** to allow students to collect their thoughts and to make certain each student has completed what she or he wishes to say. Students are taught to wait, as well. Wait time encourages students to talk and curtails your voice so you are not a domineering talker in the room.

- *Staying on topic.* Being on topic means that the central question is being addressed. Sometimes a diversionary comment will prove a fruitful avenue to explore, but teach students to keep their talk related to the topic in some way.

- *Signifying the order of speakers.* If more than one student raises a hand, you can tell the children who will speak first, second, and third. This eliminates hands waving in the air like wind-filled flags. Hand waving prevents concentration on discussion and on the planning a student needs to do before it is his or her turn to speak.

- *Permitting a child to pass.* When going around a circle to make comments or to share, "I pass" is a respected option. If you observe that a student always passes, then you can speak privately with the student and encourage the child to contribute thoughts and feelings in the future.

The climate for good discussions does not occur overnight or in the first week of school. It requires a strong feeling of community, and it will develop over time as the school year progresses. It demands consistent attention to discussion techniques by the entire group, together with strong and dependable teacher leadership.

Conclusion

Kidwatching can become central to your teaching. It just takes some work on your part to integrate it into your daily practices. Once you make the commitment to engage in this kind of observation, try out different techniques for recording what happens in your classroom—what students say, how they behave, how they interact, and perhaps what you do and say as a result. Provide yourself with the time to reflect upon what you have observed as you plan future lessons and activities.

You know that curriculum can be learned and assimilated more easily by students when they have the chance to try on new ideas and find the ones that fit them tightly like a diving suit. They need to be taught the just-right concepts and skills they can add to their knowledge base in order to flourish at their particular developmental and skill levels.

What are you doing when you are engaged in kidwatching? It is no small thing. You are attempting to understand the worldview of children, to learn where they are in the continuum of their learning, their learning style, what their interests and opinions are, and what they already know. Being knowledgeable about your students will help you plan **minilessons,** conversations, read-aloud books, student and parent conferences—your every move in the classroom. Kidwatching will help you crack open the curriculum for students.

Kidwatching works best in classrooms where the environment for responsible talk has been established. Students will not reveal their private thinking unless they are learning in a safe environment where they feel comfortable knowing that they will be seriously and respectfully treated by both their teachers and their classmates. You hope that children will invite you to join their thinking as they verbalize their feelings, reactions, concepts, or beliefs. What you learn from kidwatching and reflection will guide you toward the goal of being a more effective educator, one who has a significant impact on the lives of children.

Getting Along in the Classroom

Social and Emotional Concerns

There isn't a day that goes by in the classroom that doesn't involve a social or an emotional issue. These events may be crucial to how an individual child or the entire group functions. They often require immediate action. There is no curriculum guide that will tell you what to do, so you will need to depend on both your good instincts and your pedagogical skills.

Social and emotional problems often touch on the self-control and discipline that reside in the classroom. How you maintain discipline is a key to handling these occurrences, but *discipline* almost seems like the wrong word to use. Rather, teachers need to moderate their own behavior and language in that fine balance between authority and support. I lean in the direction of support, feeling strongly that rigid adult controls are not appropriate for young children who are learning to solve their social and emotional problems. Support encourages them to disentangle their troubles or their imagined tribulations. If any form of punishment is required, I tilt toward mild and appropriately designed reminders that make the point without belaboring the consequences.

Classroom organization resounds in these issues. They are enclosed in the structural ring you create around the classroom community. Children need to know and understand your expectations, and they need to realize that you will deal fairly with each member of the class. True, each child is an individual, but the overarching way in which you treat all the members of the group should be consistent. You cannot make any glaring exceptions because then children will notice your lapse and try to take full advantage.

You are there to support children emotionally. Of course, there is not true equity among students, because each child has very individual needs. If there is a loss in the family, you will want to be as supportive as possible. If a child is ill, you will search to find special ways to assist. If there is a separation or divorce, a child may need to rely on you for stability. Or, if a child is concerned with social relationships and hasn't learned yet to handle them well, you are there to model, coach, and support.

Whatever social or emotional problems exist, view these vignettes as broad encounters that can apply to many different circumstances. You can transfer and use the teaching strategies in other situations. And, no doubt, you will have your own tried and true methods for working with people that you have learned in your family, in school, in social organizations, and in your own very personal living situation.

"I didn't want to go to a different school."

How to help a student who moves.
- **Focus on the child**
- **Write to heal**
- **Role-play**
- **Assist new children**
- **Help the class acclimate**
- **Establish consistent expectations**
- **Consult a child study team**
- **Contact a school counselor or social worker**
- **Work with parents**

Setting the Scene

School and community: Coleytown Elementary School, Westport, Connecticut, a suburban school
Teacher: Kate Miserocchi
Description: A fourth-grade class I visited regularly while gathering material for this book

The Story

This is a tale of childhood woe. Stacy was a victim of multiple circumstances over which she had absolutely no control. Perhaps first and foremost, her parents, planning a divorce, had recently separated. In addition, the neighborhood in which Stacy lived was redistricted to a different school as part of a reorganization plan for the larger school community.

The story starts with students sitting in a circle in the meeting area. The fourth-grade classroom is unusually hushed, as if there has been a death. Preceding this quiet, there was a social eruption, with loud, distressed voices. Because Stacy seemed to be at the core of the volcanic explosion, Kate, the teacher, asks if she wishes to speak first. Tears gather behind Stacy's eyes. Everyone feels how truly distressed she is.

"I miss my friends and I miss my teacher," she cries out. "I didn't want to go to a different school."

17

Kate is shocked by the heat and fevor of the whole episode. During the past few weeks, Stacy had seemed very confident. Kate suddenly understands that perhaps the bossiness and bravura Stacy usually exhibits is a cover-up for deep emotions about the multiple changes in her life.

Kate recalls the parent conference in November. Stacy's parents had both attended a painful session. They shared the fact that during the summer they decided to separate and pursue divorce proceedings. This was an alert to look for signs of trouble; this change in family life would surely have a serious impact on Stacy. Today Stacy wants to tell the class and her teacher how she longs to return to her old school; this is the way she expresses her sadness and frustration.

The problem raised here is worth consideration because many children face the kinds of issues raised by Stacy's story. Not only was she facing a radical change in her family, but she was also trying to adjust to a new school. This double whammy is not uncommon among children, so I will suggest some helping strategies in the balance of this story under the heading of teaching strategies.

Story Background

Many children have faced moving to a new school more than once in their still-young lives. This is a tale of both city and suburban children because we live in a restless country and in restless times. A move may be occasioned by the necessities of an unstable, fluid family situation, job demands, or severe loss. As in this case, it may be a school redistricting situation. When I worked in New York City in the 1990s, children sometimes stopped coming to school without warning. Attendance rosters needed to be altered as families moved, children went to live with a different parent or caretaker, or left for reasons that were completely unknown to school authorities.

Suburban students may move away or across town. If the move is within town, parents sometimes have the option of driving their children to the old school for the balance of the year. In Stacy's case, suburban school boundaries were redrawn because of changing demographics and school construction. For example, at the present moment, my town is engaged in the nearly final stages of an extensive building program because of a burgeoning school population. Children have just been redistricted to a new middle school that opened while the old one closed to be converted to an elementary school. In Stacy's case, her neighborhood had been redistricted when an elementary school was reconditioned and reopened.

Yesterday I read a letter in a local paper from a parent whose family will probably be redistricted in two more years. Her letter, with barely concealed anger, contained a plea to other parents to join her in mounting a protest to the Board of Education over another projected change in school boundaries. Parents who feel this way will undoubtedly transfer those emotions to their children. Both parents and children are unsettled by change. Families are often extremely loyal to their local school. And even when the realignment of districts happens in an orderly, planned fashion, and when the community is aware that some children will be moved to different schools when a newly renovated building re-opens, the move is certainly not voluntary.

Though Stacy's family situation strongly affected her emotions about everything, one might have hoped nostalgia for her former school would slowly begin to dissipate after the passage of a few months. She may well have known some of her new classmates from participation on athletic teams, dance classes, the local YMCA, or other local institutions. But she was probably in an emotional place where she was unable to overcome the hurt she felt and so, on this day she directed that pain toward her school situation.

Teaching Strategies

Ralph Peterson (1992) writes that "the strength of a learning community is the ability of the members to accept one another as they are and to help one another make changes they value" (33). When trying to help a new student, he says, "caring is the thread used to weave cooperation, self-esteem, and growth of individuals and the group" (33). The important thing that happened in Stacy's classroom, on this particular morning, was that both the children and the teacher listened to her carefully, with empathy and understanding. Her words were taken at face value. The fact that her family was in turmoil was not the central issue for the classroom community. That she was confused and probably felt rejected was the point.

Focus on the Child

Stacy had many adjustments to make, including new friends, a strange school climate, perhaps a different teaching style, and changing family arrangements. The teacher, Kate, knew it was important to help Stacy feel comforted and comfortable as she tried to adjust to her new situation.

Kate began to monitor carefully the behavior of all students vis-à-vis Stacy and attend to the special needs she had at this time. She telephoned Stacy's mother, Mrs. L., that afternoon. They discussed what happened and what Stacy said about her school move. This conversation left Kate with the distinct impression that Mrs. L. could be feeding Stacy's discomfort and dissatisfaction. Kate learned that Stacy's mother was not yet at ease in the new school community. In addition, Mrs. L. gave Kate a feeling that the impending divorce had a serious impact on the emotions of both parent and child. Let's consider some specific ways you can help students like Stacy, whether their problems relate to moving, divorce, or other unknown factors that impact on the way they operate with peers.

Write to Heal
When children in your class have problems with social adjustment, you could suggest that they conduct a private correspondence or dialogue with you. The purpose of a private journal is to provide a forum for them to express their innermost feelings. The journal is seen only by you and the student writer. Confidential letters help you keep track of the pulse of a student in the hope that the discomfort she or he feels will be diminished by self-expression. Your response indicates your support as you reflect back the child's thoughts along with some simple, concrete suggestions. The fact that a child feels you are really listening is important. In Stacy's case, her teacher noted that the writing seemed honest and forthright. Stacy's need for this communication dropped off rapidly until it ceased about a month later.

You could encourage a child to write to a former teacher or to friends in the other school. This writing can be cathartic as the author expresses longing for the company of former friends. You could encourage the student to talk and write about positive experiences in the new school, or about the differences between the two schools. This letter writing will probably diminish quickly, as well. One or two letters were enough to allow Stacy to express her feelings.

Role-Play
Role-play is a technique that can help all the children in the class learn to cope with knotty social situations. You can ask for a student volunteer and quietly coach that child as the role-play proceeds. Or, you may rehearse ahead of time to help the student player become thoroughly comfortable. If you are working with a child like Stacy, the role-play can be focused on how to make friends or how to be a more cooperative class member. As you begin to feel more comfortable with role-play, you will

find its usefulness in many situations. For example, you can play the part of another student as you try to teach students how to help their classmates. In the first role-play example, the new student or aggressor will be called Student, and you will be called Helper, but the role of the teacher or helper can be played by another student.

STUDENT: I want to sit in this place.
HELPER: You always sit there. I would like that place today. Can you share it? I'd like to sit next to the teacher and you could sit on my other side.
STUDENT: I like sitting in the same place. I don't want to change.
HELPER: If you changed you would be doing me a favor. That should make you feel good.

A completely different situation could occur, one of shyness in a classroom where children are expected to take leadership roles, such as running their own book clubs. Then classmates and teacher need to help the child feel comfortable enough to try a new job.

TEACHER: Chris, I hope you will watch carefully to see what Andrew is doing to facilitate the book club. He's learned a lot about how to be a discussion leader, and I'd like to see you try doing that job in a few days.
CHRIS: I don't want to do it.
TEACHER: It's important that everyone in the classroom take a turn at doing different jobs.
CHRIS: Do I *have* to?
TEACHER: You don't have to, but I know you would do a good job and learn a lot if you tried. I will be here to help you. You can ask for help any time you need it.

Assist New Children

Most teachers have had new children join their classroom at unpredictable times during the year. When I had a classroom I always did my best to help new students feel at ease about their situation as quickly as possible. One thing I did was to assign a peer helper to the child. This classmate could explain routines, help the new student find the bathroom, the school nurse, and so on. I watched vigilantly to see that the new student was included in class conversations and recess activities, and was sitting with someone friendly at lunch. I held private, informal conversations with the new student to try and assess who he was and how he operated. I spoke with his parents quickly to gain a foothold in the way the family functioned. In other words, I did everything I could dream up to help him integrate speedily into his new learning situation.

If the child came from another school in our district, I would talk with her former teacher. Depending on the records she brought with her, I might try to reach the previous teacher, even if the student came from another state. You could even have a brief email exchange with a former teacher. A professional conversation about a new student can pay dividends in attempting to integrate that student into your classroom community.

Help the Class Acclimate

Variations of the strategies mentioned here work as you try to help all children adjust to a new class at the beginning of the year. Teachers spend the first five or six weeks of school assisting everyone become acclimated and setting the tone for the classroom community. The "one common denominator," says Donna Skolnick (2000), is "the need to belong" (53).

In September there may be several children who are new to the school. In all likelihood some students will have moved from other schools in town. Unless a teacher loops to the next grade with the entire class, children are often intermingled for the new school year, and everyone is unfamiliar with that particular group and with the teacher. By the time students reach fourth grade you hope that most of them have developed some coping skills for this experience, though this varies a great deal depending on the individual. You may have known children like Stacy who are suffering from a change in a familiar family living situation and the difficulties of learning about a new school. They deserve your special care and attention.

Establish Consistent Expectations

You will want to monitor how a new student is relating to other children. Stacy was quite heavy-handed in her peer relationships, like an aggressive forward on a hockey team. This had the unintended consequences of turning other students away from being consistent, supportive friends. When this occurs in your classroom you may decide to alert other adults who work with your students. They will want to know what you are doing to help a child like Stacy so they can help create a consistent environment for her.

Stacy had a different teacher for math, so the math teacher was apprised of her situation. Special-subject teachers—computer, physical education, and music—were made aware of Stacy's discomfort. Her classroom teacher discovered that the physical education teacher had found Stacy aggressive, asserting herself in ways that were detrimental to the smooth operation of the class. As a result, the gym teacher was happy for information she thought would assist in smoothing out the relationships in gym.

Consult a Child Study Team

At this school, a child study team meets weekly in the morning before school to discuss strategies that may help the teacher deal with children who have academic or social problems. The purpose is to support and add to the repertoire of a classroom teacher who is trying to work her way through the classroom maze of behaviors.

Kate called on the child study team for suggestions. One suggestion involved teaming Stacy with someone in the class who was a good role model. They recommended finding another student with empathy and compassion who could stand up to Stacy and be honest with her about her aggressive behavior. Kate selected Eve, who fit this description. She spoke first with Eve. As they talked about what Stacy had said about her old school and her friends, the idea of helping appealed to Eve. Then Kate spoke with Stacy about how consoling it would be to have a supportive friend.

Finally, Kate spoke with Eve and Stacy together and suggested times when they could work as partners during class. She explained to both of them that Eve could help Stacy just as she had asked another student to help John four weeks ago when he came from a different town. This was intended to ease Stacy's anxieties, and she seemed willing to accept Eve's support.

Contact a School Counselor or Social Worker

Stacy's problem ran deeper than simply being in a new school. Schools have different professionals who may be able to play a role in assisting a child like this. Because Stacy has the long-term problem of divorce together with her natural tendencies to be domineering, the counselor or social worker might meet with a peer group that included Stacy. Stacy could come away from such sessions feeling much more positive toward her new school. Longer-term counseling, perhaps individual sessions, would help her cope with the family situation.

Work with Parents

Continuing with Stacy as our example, a face-to-face conversation with a parent could help alleviate specific problems. You might encourage

Stacy's mother to facilitate her friendship with children like Eve. Her mother could encourage after-school activities or invite Eve to dinner. By the time a child is in fourth grade, parents cannot play too active a role in social arrangements. A lot needs to be left to the children, but Stacy's mother might make it easier for Stacy to think about classmates and friends if Stacy felt positive about the new school. Stacy is not limited to those fourth graders in her own classroom, of course. She may wish to branch out to children she meets from the other classes.

Depending on how your relationship develops, you may feel comfortable speaking with the mother about her own attitudes toward the redistricting. Perhaps she was one of the people, like the letter writer mentioned earlier, who opposed the change in districts and had been verbal about it in front of her children. Since parents and children do not have any control over something like a school realignment, it is certainly not positive for adults to play a negative role. Their children pick up on their attitudes and internalize them. You will be doing something very constructive if you help a parent find positive things about the new school that she can share with her daughter.

Conclusion

I have written about Stacy because a situation, with variations on this theme, can occur in your classroom at any time. New children, who feel uncomfortable for whatever reason need the tender, loving care of their teacher and classmates. Learning is more difficult when a student is angry or frustrated. Because motivation is much stronger after a certain comfort level is reached, you will want to help all your students reach a feeling of ease and safety in your classroom. Everyone needs to pull together to help new children become calm enough to accept the learning environment in which they are immersed.

A nine-year-old student is mature enough to maintain some friends from the old school, especially when it is in the same town, and add to her social life by blending in new friends almost like you fold in egg whites to make a smooth cake batter. By teaching coping mechanisms to children like Stacy, you will help them adjust to the new environments they may face at other times throughout their lives. Your goal is to teach them to be cooperative, constructive members of all the future communities in which they will live. You are teaching specific skills for a lifetime of use.

"My mom buys me things because she wants me to stop bothering her."

How to help children modify self-defeating behavior.

- **Encourage**
- **Be specific**
- **Establish logical and consistent consequences**
- **Talk it out**
- **Work with parents**

Setting the Scene

School and community: Coleytown Elementary School, Westport, Connecticut, a suburban school

Teacher: Whitney McCarthy

Description: Self-contained first-grade classroom with special education students mainstreamed; I visited on a regular basis to gather material for this book

The Story

First graders discuss their weekend. Charles is very charged up because, as he is telling his friends, he got a new basketball shirt. He is wearing it—a shiny blue shirt that has the name of his favorite player on the front and that player's number in large letters on the back. It is very flashy.

Charles says loudly, bragging a bit, "My mom didn't want to buy it. She thought it was too expensive. But I pestered and pestered her. Finally she got it. She buys me things because she wants me to stop bothering her."

Other students chime in. Some say their mothers and fathers never buy things if they are a pest. Several nod in assent to Charles. They know the feeling of getting something after causing a ruckus. There is a difference of attitudes among the children, just as there must be a variety of responses from parents when children want something they don't want to give them. As I listen it occurs to me that I have heard this kind

26

*"My mom buys
me things because
she wants me to
stop bothering
her."*

of talk in years past, and that this learned behavior from home can spill into the classroom. It is school-related because whatever way children learn to act at home to achieve their goals, they quite comfortably reenact in the classroom. This section is not just about children who pester their parents for possessions, it is also about children who have learned to behave in any self-centered or self-defeating way. Those students will need your guidance if they are to live as constructive and cooperative members in your classroom community.

On this particular morning Whitney, the teacher, takes a strong and forthright stance. She explains to her students that when her daughter, Gretchen, gets whiny or pesky there are definite consequences. Whitney and Ted, her husband, definitely do not respond by doing what Gretchen wants. In fact, quite the opposite. They present a united front and what Gretchen is requesting is off the table, at least for the moment.

Story Background

The scenery for this story is sketched in child development. Brazelton and Greenspan (2000) explain, "As children move through their seventh and eighth years, their horizons expand. Their world is other kids. They begin to move from the family-oriented stage of development and enter the multifaceted world of their peers, moving into the politics of the playground" (121).

Penelope Leach (1994) states that "In theory, commercial and societal values need not conflict because people do not have to buy what they do not want, and parents, holders of the purchasing power, do not have to buy for children what they do not want them to have. In practice, though, there is conflict and it haunts many families. The advertising arm of commerce does not simply ask people what they want or show them what there is: it teaches them what to want" (155).

It is obvious that when children know they can bother their parents to achieve certain results, they will extend those tactics to both teachers and friends. Since you need to be deeply concerned with the social atmosphere in your classroom, you must, of necessity, be troubled when you witness a child doing his level best to reach certain ends with the use of inappropriate behavior. The question becomes, what can you do about it?

In *Positive Discipline,* Jane Nelson (1987) gives us guidelines for reacting to children who misbehave. The first thing to consider is that they are social beings. "Children make decisions about themselves and how to behave, based on how they see themselves in relationship to others and how they *think* others feel about them" (23). Perhaps Charles pestered his mother to purchase the basketball shirt he thought he needed because someone else had one, or maybe he wanted it to impress his peers. Nelson continues that "behavior is goal oriented. Often children are not consciously aware of the goal they hope to achieve" (23). Charles may not have realized that he wanted to impress people with his shirt; he was only aware of the fact that he really, passionately wanted it.

Teaching Strategies

Nelson gives us guidance for how to support children as they work to change their behavior. She suggests that there are four steps for gaining cooperation: "(a) Guess how [your] child is feeling. Get into the child's world. Check . . . to see if your guess is correct. (b) Show understanding . . . If possible share an example of a time when you felt the same. (c) Share your feelings about the situation. (d) Work together on ideas to avoid the problem in the future" (xix).

Leach notes that "Self-discipline is a slow-growing plant that roots in children's identification with parents or parent substitutes. Learning how to behave—and to be more comfortable behaving that way—depends on parental influence rather than power, on the warmth of the relationship adults offer rather than the clarity of the orders they impose" (117). With that in mind, you will find some concrete suggestions in this section to help you deal with a myriad of behavioral problems. The important thing is to be evenhanded and calm with students who have learned unusual or unacceptable ways of achieving their goals. As Leach tells us, you will want to remember that "learning acceptable behavior is more difficult and takes longer than learning a specific skill because what has to be learned is complex, involves control of powerful impulses, and often demands that children act against what they see as their own best interests" (119).

Encourage

Children need encouragement to confirm the kind of behaviors that are socially acceptable. Many teachers use positive talk. You might quietly say something like "I notice that Steven is sitting quietly, ready to listen." Avoid using negative comments, such as "I'm waiting for everyone to get quiet," or raising your voice to state "You're too noisy."

Another way to give encouragement is to make quiet, private comments to individual children at unexpected times, such as when they are walking to lunch or leaving the classroom for the afternoon. You could

*"My mom buys
me things because
she wants me to
stop bothering
her."*

put your arm around a youngster and say, "You did a good job getting ready for our meeting today. I noticed how you picked up math materials and helped put them away." This type of comment goes a very long way with most children.

Some students are accustomed to receiving strongly disapproving notice from their parents. They hear so much of it that they may seek it from other adults. If you are working with a child like this, you will find that avoiding negative talk or ignoring the more benign negative behavior may help turn the child around and assist her in being ready to receive positive comments from you when they are warranted. Even the smallest positive talk will surprise and support this kind of child.

Be Specific

Students need to know exactly how you will handle disciplinary situations and what to expect when something arises that calls for your authority. Vivian Paley (1992) states that "We must be told, when we are young, what rules to live by" (110). At the beginning of a school year, you will want to spell out exactly how you will handle behavior that is unacceptable. You will need to repeat your limits and rules whenever necessary and be willing to act on them. If a child like Charles feels that he can bend the edges to get what he wants, he will soon learn that he is not able to do this at school if you are consistent as you spell out and carry through on your expectations.

In many classrooms, the students and teacher develop a list of rules or expectations during the first days of school in the late summer. These rules are written on a **reference chart** and posted on the wall in the classroom—a classroom constitution. You may find that you want to add to these rules during the year. They can be a great help in enforcing the code of behavior. You can simply point to the rule when a child needs a reminder, which helps you avoid repeating it in a voice that could sound annoyed.

Establish Logical and Consistent Consequences

If you want to achieve certain behaviors, then logical consequences will help. For example, when a child cannot settle down for the morning's work, you may ask him to take a brief time-out away from the group. The other day I heard Sarah Spencer, a fourth-grade teacher, say, in almost a monotone voice, "Jen, take a break." Jen got up from her seat, left the group, and went to sit quietly in a separate, established part of the room for a few minutes. It was the third week of school. The reason this worked so well is that the entire school is using the same language for discipline.

If you work in a setting where there isn't consistency from class to class, then you will have to be even more firm and explicit. Applying rules quietly and consistently will become easier after examples have been set in the classroom. But it will not work if you ask students to take logical consequences in the morning but don't bother with them in the afternoon as you wear down. It is important to be consistent about what you require children to do and how you ask them to do it.

Not only should consequences be consistent, but they also should be logical. If a child needs to modify his behavior about how he acts in the group, a time-out may seem appropriate. If another student needs help remembering to bring her homework, some small additional homework that evening will help her remember in the future. If a child has trouble controlling his behavior on the playground, perhaps he needs to stay beside the supervising teacher for a short time until he can play well with his friends. I wouldn't keep him off the playground, because he needs to breathe fresh air and use his large muscles. I am not speaking here about grandiose or long-lasting punishments, but something that is noticeable and logical for children.

Talk It Out

The boys and girls in your classroom want to be treated with respect. Talking about a problem is recommended as a strategy to pursue. Dealing out consequences when a child doesn't understand why she has received them is unfair and probably meaningless. It may be important to take a few minutes to explain privately to a child why you are asking her to take time-out, or sit separately from the group, or do a few extra math problems. Talking things over privately is preferred to public comments in front of the entire group. Your purpose is to help a student achieve a better set of behaviors, not to embarrass or shame.

Class meetings can help to inform everyone about problems and serve as a time to talk over possible solutions. You may wish to consult Nelson's book *Positive Discipline* for suggestions about running a regular class meeting. When I had my own classroom, we had a weekly meeting, mostly to resolve the social problems that cropped up naturally. These class meetings gave the children the opportunity to talk through their concerns and come to some consensus about how to smooth out what they perceived as trouble. I found them well worth the time they took. Jane Nelson's book gives specific suggestions about how to set the agenda, conduct the meeting, and come to some agreement about solutions.

Work with Parents

Your school probably has a regular time of year for parent conferences, but in some cases it is best not to wait until scheduled conferences to talk with parents about a child's behavior. A face-to-face conference early in the school year, after you feel sure of your ground, will bring its own rewards. I have found that most often when I have dreaded a conference because I felt I needed to talk about behavioral problems and worried about what the parent might feel or say, the surprise was that the parent was already very much aware of those behaviors. You may be confirming what the parent knows from home or from talking with last year's teacher. A parent is usually grateful for suggestions about ways that the two of you can work together to help a child.

If you both work consistently on a set of problems or behaviors, you will achieve much better and faster results. Children need consistent expectations, and when the schoolroom and the home are requiring the same things and have similar goals, it will be more beneficial. You don't want to set up a situation where the child is living with one set of expectations at home and another at school. This is terribly confusing.

Another way to work with parents is to use the telephone or e-mail, if you have it. This works best after a face-to-face dialogue has been established. You can provide positive reinforcement for a child who has met your goals on any particular day, or during the week. I often picked up the telephone to leave a quick message for a parent saying that their child had worked hard toward a specific goal, such as being a good listener that week. This was an effective way of communicating with parents and reinforcing good behavior for children. Brief written notes are helpful, too. In all these examples, the child should know ahead of time that you are phoning or what is contained in a note so that you are reinforcing better behavior.

Conclusion

As Brazelton and Greenspan note, "Children and adolescents must have a sense of protection and ongoing nurturing relationships as well as structure. . . . Expectations born out of interactions with adults and the development of real skills are essential in providing opportunities for growth and development" (158). The central point of this vignette is that you are attempting to work toward the point where each child is capable of regulating his impulses and controlling his behavior in an appropriate manner.

Life in school will be a lot more joyful if you can help your students achieve good self-discipline and you don't feel that you are walking around carrying the big stick, constantly involved with discipline. Children who live in a consistent, quiet, and pleasurable environment that is developmentally appropriate and joyful will respond to the expectations of the teacher and the school community. Don Graves (2001) indicated in a talk to Westport, Connecticut, staff that "We need to be ready to spot that special thing." When you do look for those unusual possibilities, he explained, children "can send energy back to you." The implication was that how children are viewed goes a long way toward solving behavior problems.

A lot depends on your attitude. I have a friend who always said the present year was the best one she had ever had. She is just that kind of person. And the school year was the best ever because she thought it was and expected it to be. When I was doing staff development, I knew teachers who always talked about how the present class was the worst one they had ever had, the one that drove them crazy—and, as you would expect, each year it was like that. Children act the way they are expected to perform. They rise to the occasion or sink to the depths.

Being honest, being consistent, having a sense of humor, enjoying your days in the classroom, enforcing the few rules you develop together with your students—all of these things will make your job more pleasurable and will help your students learn all the wonderful things you have to offer them.

Partner and Group Work

The two vignettes that follow present a common theme. They speak to the concerns of students about working with partners or in small groups. The teaching strategies in one vignette can be transferred to the problems presented in the other, and to different problems you may have in your classroom. These vignettes attempt to highlight student concerns and thinking about the social skills that impact on group tasks at school, and how to resolve or ameliorate the problems that arise when students work in groups.

In his book *Life in a Crowded Place: Making a Learning Community,* Ralph Peterson (1992) tells us that "In discussion, students always focus their attention on some 'thing' in order to know and understand. Judgments are made, ideas are reflected upon, points are debated, propositions are proven, and conclusions are sought" (49). As the teacher, you plan for group work because you believe in its power and importance. Because you believe students learn from each other and from group transactions, you structure frequent opportunities for discussion and the processing of information in both large and small groups. You plan for peer conferences. You institute book discussion groups. You spend time debriefing with your whole class after students have worked in smaller clusters. You hold class meetings in which students can express their opinions and come to a conclusion about something that is important to all of you.

"What if the discussion leader is bossy?"

How to help students work productively in groups.
- **Discuss reading preferences**
- **Determine student responsibilities**
- **Explore the problem**

Setting the Scene

School and community: Coleytown Elementary School, Westport, Connecticut, a suburban school district

Teachers: Kate Miserocchi and Sarah Spencer

Description: Two fourth-grade classes where teachers team-teach for reading; I visited regularly to gather information for this book

The Story

In these fourth grades, Sarah Spencer and Kate Miserocchi team-teach the reading workshop. It is January and they begin to organize forty-five students into groups of "reading friends," the term they use for book clubs. They want students to know more about the reading preferences of classmates before forming the groups of reading friends that will integrate both classrooms.

Each child has prepared a short presentation to acquaint other students with her reading interests and habits. The plan is to have children select members for their student-led literature circles after these talks. Students have been asked to include the following information:

- Titles of books recently enjoyed
- Favorite reading genre(s)
- Information about reading habits, including where and when they do most of their reading
- Other information that is important for peers to know about the student's reading life

Before individual presentations begin, the two classes gather together in a large circle on the floor. Sarah asks students if they have any

questions about what they are going to do, and several children raise
their hands to ask the following questions:

- Why are we doing these speeches?
- What does that mean—a reading friend?
- Why should we have reading friends?

Students request explicit information about the teachers' intentions,
and these queries are answered in detail. The explanations appear to sat-
isfy the students, who settle back to listen.

Some children have prepared note cards for their talk; others are
ready to speak extemporaneously. Many have rehearsed and appear quite
self-confident as they describe their reading habits and interests. They
have decided to take turns alphabetically. Each student sits with a clipboard that has an alphabetized class list, together with space after each
name for note taking. (See Figure 6.) Students are instructed to record
information that will assist them in the selection of their reading
friends.

As each child speaks, the teachers listen and closely watch how
notes are being made. It soon becomes obvious that students are writing
information about their friends, and leaving blank spaces following the
names of classmates with whom they have no interest in working. A message is being broadcast as if the volume of a stereo system were turned
to the highest point. Students have taken the title announced by their
teachers, *reading friends,* literally. They prefer to work with their social
friends.

At lunch, Kate, Sarah, and I consider the session and share our observations. Upon reflection, we agree that it seems developmentally appropriate for fourth graders to focus on friends and social groups as they
consider which students they want to work with in their book clubs.
Sarah remarks that this speaks to her past experience—that it is important for the eventual outcome of the book clubs to follow the lead of the
children and allow for student choice both in creating and implement-
ing the book clubs.

Story Background

The emphasis on choice and the allowance of time for talk among students comes directly out of the research that began to hold sway in the
1980s. This research has been followed up more recently and discussed
in a variety of professional books.

Ms. Miserocchi's Class
Jamie Austen
Jesse Brown
Tim Downing
Adam French
Emily Green
Deborah Howe
James Hunt
Dexter Lance
Reed Luftow
Liza Pinto
Kathryn Rowley
Nick Ryan
Jana Schaffer
Carol Sharp
Frank Tibbets
Ann Watson

FIGURE 6 Class list

Joanne Hindley (1996) reports to us that her third-grade students made a list of the important factors in selecting a book group. Here is the chart they made:

I would choose

- someone who is a friend, that you like to hang out with
- someone who likes the same authors you do
- a person who likes to read the same type of books, like mysteries or nonfiction
- someone who also likes a certain series
- someone who would want to read all the books in a series
- someone who wants to reread books
- someone who likes different kinds of books than you do so you'll read new things. (132)

The reading talks by the fourth graders in this vignette drew upon experiences from earlier in the year. For example, in September each student had constructed a poster of his personal reading time line. This poster featured information about his reading life, including memories of being read to as a toddler and preschool child, memories of learning to read, reading habits he had developed, favorite books, and other information he considered relevant. The posters were shared and discussed in class before they were displayed in the hallway. Later, students interviewed their parents to find out what genres they enjoyed reading and discover the titles of their favorite books. They held classroom conversations about parental preferences, putting the information on reference charts, and the teachers shared details about their own reading lives during these discussions.

Teaching Strategies

The speeches about reading preferences opened up new lines of talk that Kate and Sarah decide to pursue. Peterson and Eeds (1990) say that they do this very same thing: "We don't work out in advance what is going to happen when we teach. Instead, we prepare ourselves carefully to respond to what *might* happen within a living encounter. We rely on timing and our ability to seize the moment . . ." (15).

Having observed the note-taking behavior, Kate and Sarah decide to introduce an additional step before organizing and launching the book clubs. The next day students sit in the large circle again, and teachers share what they observed while the students were making notes. They tell the group that they want to honor what they observed and try to organize the reading friend groups according to the students' expressed wishes—that the students care about being in book clubs with classmates with whom they feel comfortable and with whom they can work well, just as adults create book clubs with their friends.

Discuss Reading Preferences

Kate and Sarah ask students to tell the group in detail who they want to work with because of a common interest in the same genre, series, or author. For example, in the previous meeting Dexter said he liked to read Walter Dean Myers and Reed talked about the Redwall series written by Brian Jacques. Each had mentioned a classmate who shared these interests. Today, as the fourth graders go around the circle to talk about authors and genres and which students they believe they can work with, everyone speaks and listens respectfully. They seem acutely aware of the fact that they are taking responsibility for putting themselves into groups of reading friends.

Kate stands at the chart stand to record each child's name next to a genre, author, or series as it is mentioned. When a second, third, or fourth student cites duplicate information, her name is added in the appropriate place. At the end of the period it is abundantly clear how to organize the groups. Because the teachers prefer groups of four or five members at most, some topics of interest require more than one reading friends group in order to make the book clubs a workable size. The first meeting, when the students talked about reading habits and genres, is not wasted; now everyone is aware of preferences and the work goes quickly. The close, sensitive teacher observation has led to a system that will help achieve the goal of well-oiled teams for the reading friends work.

Decide Student Responsibilities

Students understand that they are expected to read their books at home as homework and come to class prepared to hold discussions with their reading friends. Some students have worked in book clubs in other classrooms, though most have not. Sarah and Kate feel they need to be more specific about their expectations for how the book clubs will function. Along with **choice,** they want to build in responsibility and accountability.

Sarah takes the lead. She speaks about defining jobs that will expedite the smooth operation of the book clubs. She begins, "Each time your reading friends group meets you will have fifteen to twenty minutes in class to discuss what you have read. What jobs will you need to make this work for you?" To assist their thinking, Sarah begins the list by suggesting the necessity of a discussion leader. She explains what such a job would entail. The class settles on the following list:

- *Discussion Leader* keeps the conversation going and keeps everyone on task.
- *Recorder* writes a summary at the end of the meeting and shares the group's discussion with the whole class.
- *Secretary* keeps a list of possible books to read.
- *Topic or Question Leader* makes certain everyone is responsible and prepared for the questions to be discussed.
- *Caller* is responsible for telephoning group members at home to remind them of their nightly reading assignment and the topic they agreed to discuss the following day.
- *Vocabulary Keeper* records a list of unfamiliar words.

After further discussion, students decide that the secretary could do the calling, so those two jobs are combined into one and the name is revised to *book secretary,* leaving five jobs. In some groups, one person will need to do more than one job or they will have to omit certain jobs, since several groups are composed of only three people. These decisions are left to the students. (Once they met in their groups, some students changed the jobs around anyway and revised the list to make it work for their particular group.)

Everything seems ready to go, and excitement is building. Suddenly, Deborah raises her hand to ask a socially appropriate question. Referring back to the job of discussion leader, she asks what will happen if, as she puts it, "the discussion leader is bossy." Her question may be on the minds of many children as she draws on her social experiences to anticipate a frequent problem among nine-year-olds. The teachers immediately realize that this question needs to be addressed by the entire group. They decide to set aside time to talk about this before the book club work gets underway in an attempt to prevent future problems.

Explore the Problem

Book club participants are divided into two groups, one to meet in Kate's classroom, the other in Sarah's. The group in Kate's room will discuss Deborah's concerns, while the other students read and talk about a nonfiction article with Sarah's student teacher, Susan Ostopow. Another day, Kate and Sarah will meet with the balance of the students while the first group reads the article with Susan.

I agree to lead this session because Kate and Sarah want the opportunity to play different roles. Sarah will sit at the computer and record the talk for future examination, and Kate will sit in the group as an observer. I initiate the discussion with a review of the jobs the students agreed upon. I remark that it would help the smooth operation of the book clubs if we explore Deborah's question about bossiness before they get under way.

JANE: Deborah said that she didn't like the idea of having a discussion leader because she was worried about how that person might act.

[I ask Deborah to elaborate her thinking for the group.]

DEBORAH [with obvious disdain]: I was thinking that the discussion leader would think they are the boss of the whole group.

JANE: Let's talk about this because Deborah is right; the group won't work well if someone is being bossy. Does anyone have suggestions about what you can do if the discussion leader is interfering with the way the group functions?

DEBORAH: You don't have to tell a teacher. They might get upset. You could ask [the student] to stop talking about the subject and if they don't, get a teacher.

[I use an extended wait time to give students the opportunity to join the discussion, but no other children seem willing to contribute at this point.]

JANE: I'm thinking of a sports analogy. Raise your hand if you play team sports. [Most hands go up.] What do you do if there is a problem with the way someone is behaving on your team? It seems to me this could be similar.

NICK: Our team never has any problems.

KATHRYN: You should figure it out and talk to each other about it. If someone is being bossy, you should tell them. You should do everything you can and the last thing is to go to a grown-up.

JAMIE: Talk to each other and try to work it out. It would be good to apologize and cooperate.

[As this vein seems exhausted, I turn the conversation a bit.]

JANE: What's your major goal with your reading friends? Why are you having book clubs?

LIZA: It teaches you to work in a group. If someone doesn't like [what is happening], we work it out.

The discussion goes on. It veers in a new direction as students begin to grapple with what to do if there are varying opinions about a book. Kathryn remarks that you "can't fight with an opinion. There isn't a right or wrong." At the end, however, Deborah asks another show stopper question: "What if one person wants to quit the book?"

It is clear to the three teachers present that additional questions like this one will arise as the student-led literature circles proceed, but students are so anxious to begin that it seems appropriate to move on to the next phase and deal with problems later. Subsequent decisions can be made public to the whole group so that each group of reading friends is empowered to ride as smoothly as possible over the inevitable bumps in the road. With the idea of moving ahead, James suggests that recorders keep track of problems that could be shared with the larger group. Then the teachers could either teach minilessons or hold discussions as they judge best. These fourth graders are ready to begin the work with their reading friends.

Conclusion

How does this story instruct? Sensitive kidwatching coupled with intense reflection can guide teachers toward appropriate responses. Sometimes you may need to slow down and take the time to do additional teaching before forging ahead with new reading or writing work. In this case, first Kate and Sarah noticed the note taking their students were doing and then they acted on that information by rethinking the formation of the book clubs. Next, they engaged their students in conversations over the social concerns Deborah expressed.

Careful preparation to structure partner and group work is important if that work is to be successful. Since you try to set up group work to become a positive learning experience, you will want to help children learn to resolve the interpersonal problems that necessarily arise. These fourth graders talked about how important it is to solve problems themselves, to address them directly with the peer who is causing them discomfort, and to ask for teacher involvement only after their own efforts have failed. But being able to verbalize this doesn't mean they can implement these strategies skillfully. In my experience, students have a strong desire to discuss this kind of problem, to air their feelings, and to get additional help and reinforcement from adults, but they cannot always follow up on what they are able to verbalize.

From your own social experiences, you will understand that there is no standard answer for problems that arise in personal relationships. A tough knot that can be untied one way in one situation may never arise in exactly the same configuration again. Solutions need to be revised for the next problem. As the adult in the classroom, you can encourage, teach, and model for children as they grapple with age-appropriate social problems. At the same time, try not to solve these problems for them with authoritarian directives.

Children need to identify and practice solutions to social problems on their own. As Brazelton and Greenspan explain, "The ability to diagnose group dynamics helps children to develop cognitive and social skills that will be very valuable in school—and beyond school, in the real world. They learn that most of life operates in shades of gray, not in all-or-nothing extremes" (122).

Several ideas come to mind to assist children with interpersonal problems:

- Hold a class meeting to discuss problems either before or as they arise.
- Role-play, either with the teacher taking one role or with two or three students modeling for everyone as the teacher coaches.
- Revisit a social situation to reinforce learning, using both oral and visual aids to assist different types of learners.
- Use appropriate literature to focus on social problems.
- Model social situations as you talk with colleagues while students listen (a **fishbowl activity**).

Whatever you do, no matter how much you work, you cannot assume that group work will go without a hitch. Your job is to help children as often and as deeply as you can, giving them opportunities for practice and occasions to discuss what has happened. This social mission is every bit as important as your other teaching, and it is one that recurs like a well-worn theme throughout the year and through all the grades.

"He didn't listen to me."

How to ease the inevitable problems that develop in partner work.

- **Invite student suggestions**
- **Take additional time to prepare**
- **Develop future cooperation**

Setting the Scene

School and community: Coleytown Elementary School, Westport, Connecticut, a suburban district

Teachers: Mara Schwartz and Nancy Kovacic

Description: This story takes place in Mara's second-grade classroom as her students are joined by third graders from Nancy's room for writing workshop partner work; I visited Mara's room regularly to do research for this book

The Story

Third graders come quietly into the classroom and settle with the second graders in the meeting area. None of the students have been in this classroom before since it is Mara's first year to teach second grade. All these children have been working with writing partners within their respective classrooms. Now, Nancy and Mara state their intentions clearly: They think it would help students to have new writing partners, who will assist each other with fresh ideas and be able to brainstorm how to solve any problems writers are having. The teachers give specific directions and announce the partnerships they have already arranged. (Nancy and Mara had met to set up the partners, mainly based on the topics children had chosen, such as writing about dogs.)

Since the children have had extensive practice working with peer writing partners, the teachers feel the students understand how to do this work. They ask students to spend some time getting to know each other first, and they model sample conversations. Next, they ask the children to take turns reading their pieces to each other. After the children get acquainted and share, the teachers believe that the students should be ready to help each other with writing.

Boys and girls locate their assigned partners and move to tables around the room. Some look a bit unsure while others happen to be working with friends. Mara and Nancy move around the room to answer questions, listen, and give assistance where needed. They naturally focus on students who may have difficulty with this activity, and Mara asks me to begin with two boys she feels might need some adult help and supervision.

I scan the room. It is clear that some of the partnerships are working well while other children are sitting as if alone. The variety of scenarios in the classroom mirror those you would see if these groups were working in their own classrooms. The teachers have been unable to give everyone a peer who is writing on the same topic, and there is a wide range of writing and social skills.

I am sitting alongside Ethan and Keith. They could be toddlers engaged in parallel play. Ethan is writing about snowboarding, and Keith's piece is about adopting a dog from the local pound. They seem uncomfortable in this new situation and are ignoring each other. They need adult help. I suggest they talk more about their topics. They clearly need to know more about each other, and I try to launch them on a partnership.

I move across the room to Eve and Pam. They are also writing about different topics, but they have managed to bond into a cooperative relationship in a very short time. Pam demonstrates how she makes a story map to search for ideas about her central **seed** idea. Eve has never seen this and is clearly intrigued, asking Pam some excellent questions. Pam guides Eve as she maps her thoughts before she begins to write any new material.

The period flies by for the young writers who are constructively engaged in their work. For students like Ethan and Keith, however, it may feel endless. Mara asks the children to stop and give feedback to their partners about what they have observed during this process, or to talk about how they feel about this work together. Kat, Mary, and Rena, a threesome, get into a lively discussion. Rena, a second grader, takes the lead, saying, "You inspired me by showing me how you moved text around. I think I'm going to try that."

The meeting of the two classes is over, and the third graders get ready to return to their own classroom. After they leave, Mara gathers her students on the rug. As soon as they settle down and are ready to listen, she asks, "How was this experience for you?" They are eager to talk. Their answers are diverse, but the theme that becomes dominant is voiced by Donald: "He didn't listen." There is a strong, pulsating drumbeat about the lack of cooperation or courtesy as students assess the past forty-five minutes.

Story Background

There are several models of teaching at Coleytown Elementary School. Among those models, some teachers work in partnerships across grades. A few do team-teaching within one grade. Some loop with their students to the next grade. Mara, the second-grade teacher, and Nancy, the teacher of third grade, both had self-contained classes, and on the day I am writing about, they joined their classes for the first time to do peer conferencing. They wanted to cross-fertilize ideas between the two classes and grades. Part of their purpose was to place children in the teaching role to help them reinforce and strengthen their skills by teaching a peer.

I am able to write more detail about Mara's class because I was a regular visitor there and knew the students well as writers. These boys and girls had been writing intensely in their notebooks. Mara taught a wide variety of minilessons to give students a range of ideas for notebook entries. She provided them with a rich diet of picture books as well. For weeks they collected entries in their notebooks. There was palpable excitement in the room on the day they began to reread their notebooks to make a decision about a seed idea that was important enough to inspire their work on a re-envisioned piece of writing. Nancy's class was going through the same process. They were at the point of beginning to write entries around their seed ideas, not quite as far along in the process as the second graders.

Katie Wood Ray (1999) explains the same type of instruction that Mara and Nancy were providing: "Our goal in this teaching was to help the students take the material they had gathered around their seed ideas and read like writers to find possibilities for how they might draft those ideas and write well" (52). It was easy to visualize how talking with a partner might support the writing and supply students with new writing ideas.

Teaching Strategies

Nancy's class has departed. Mara asks her class how they would assess the work time with the third graders. The children respond to Mara's question in two very diverse ways. First, there is a chorus of "he didn't listen," "he wouldn't stop humming," or "she didn't pay any attention to me." These comments erupt like fresh chicken pox sores when one student introduces the virus. In contrast, others quietly say that they enjoyed this partner work with different writers, they made a new friend, or they got some good, fresh ideas. However, the infection is so virulent that even Rena, who sounded so positive when her threesome was giving each other feedback, makes a one-hundred-eighty-degree turn to join the naysayers. Mara wisely decides she will take cues from her own observations and moves to wrap up the evaluation session.

The negative student feelings do reinforce some of Mara's impressions as she was circulating in the room during the partner work; she is not satisfied with the way things went. Perhaps that dissatisfaction is what prompted her original question, though she regularly asked children to assess a class period. She had hoped for more give-and-take between the second and third graders. Her expectations were based on the kind of intense and constructive sharing her students do with their classmates during writers' workshop. She may have underestimated the hard, successful work she had done to scaffold peer writing conferences since September. Or, she may have underestimated the impact that getting acquainted with new partners would have.

Invite Student Suggestions

Mara tries to focus on the voices of those who have positive things to say. This prompts her to ask the next question, "If we do this again, and I don't know if we will, how would you improve it?" Now the second graders switch to make some constructive and thoughtful suggestions:

RENA: I think we should circle up first and then everyone say something to interest each other and then do the match. [In other words, teachers would not do the partner matching first without student input.]

MARK: Let us choose. If you know someone and can work with them, we could choose that person as a partner.

PAM: I think we should talk with our partner about a problem if that happens. If she is interrupting or not listening, we should talk to her.

MARA [to wrap up the discussion]: I would want you to have more time to get to know each other on the first day. Then on a different day you could do some work together.

It is clear that Mara felt there would be advantages to giving students more time to become acquainted. Extra time would have been worthwhile even for the partners who worked together well, but especially for those who had less in the way of social skills or less to contribute to a peer writing conference. My own experiences of matching second graders and kindergarten students as writing partners taught me that it takes time to develop the relationships and skills that children can gain from this kind of work. When Hilda Rhodes and I established writing partners between our students in the early 1990s, we found it worthwhile to schedule partner work every other week throughout the school year.

Take Additional Time to Prepare

The difficulty with planning an additional class period with a more social focus is that teachers feel so pressured about how they use every minute of class time. If partner work is valued and teachers feel their students can learn from children in another class, then time is required to set the stage with detailed scenery. Nancy and Mara did a careful planning job for this lesson, but unanticipated or unavoidable things developed in this first experience between the two classes. They were:

- Unavoidably, each class was in a different place on the continuum of notebook writing.
- Each teacher had her own individual teaching style that was, of course, different.
- Second graders may have anticipated more help and respect than they could receive from third graders.
- Pairing by writing theme may have overlooked individual social difficulties.
- A first-time experience is bound to have rough edges. More practice and better acquaintance is needed for smoother sailing.

The second graders seemed critical, even resistant, because they were accustomed to working with a partner in their own class, where the issues of getting to know each other no longer remained. Implied in the seven-year-olds' comments was an air of offense. They may have assumed that eight-year-olds would be more grown up. They did not realize that third graders are only one year away from second grade in skill and maturity. They are not the very mature people that second graders may assume them to be!

Develop Future Cooperation

Having begun this partnership between the two classes, it could be helpful to continue the cooperation. This would encourage more comfortable and respectful relationships. One short meeting of the two classes is not enough to develop the kind of sharing and communication that both students and teachers would like to see. The partnerships introduced by these two experienced teachers between second and third graders will remain as hard and green as a fruit picked too early unless this work is carried forward and refined. Two teachers interested in the benefits of cross-fertilization may wish to consider a long-term partnership between their students.

Conclusion

There are challenges to structuring partner and group work. The goal of having children work with peers to discuss their ideas and work is an important and often fascinating one. The benefits of skilled group work for students are clear. For example, the best way to learn something is to teach it to someone else. When Pam showed Eve how to use a graphic organizer, she solidified her understanding of that technique and made it a firmer part of her own repertoire. By having discussions with reading friends, participating in peer writing conferences, and talking about which notebook entries might contain seeds for a meaningful piece to publish, students have the opportunity to solidify and extend their skills as well as to hear fresh ideas.

Mara and Nancy had a fine idea when they set out to weave their two classes together for writing conferences. It takes time for children to develop relationships that help them talk fruitfully with each other, and there will always be some children for whom this strategy is not as productive as you might hope. My focus would be on the comments of the children who found this a positive experience. The classes can move on from there.

It is clear that by the age of seven many children have answers for how to solve social or behavioral problems, but they need a great deal of practice to implement those ideas. To unlock the secrets and teach around the problems of group or partner work, you will find it helpful to follow Mara's lead and ask, "How did it go for you today? Do you have any suggestions?" You will want to provide opportunities so your students can learn social strategies, practice them, plant their learning in firmer soil, and air their appraisals of the interpersonal activities you structure. You cannot take for granted that after several experiences this work is finished or accomplished, and that you have empowered them to move forward alone. You will want to continue guiding them as they learn, practice, and hone their cooperative skills.

Classroom Organization and Management 2

A Responsive Curriculum

As I listened to children while doing research for this book, I heard comments and questions from them that were universal, transcending grade level, time, and location. No doubt they are similar to ones that you grapple with frequently. Suggestions for solving these problems are not provided in any curriculum guide. Personal concerns and queries are part of an informal curriculum that is not written down or spelled out anywhere. They are connected to the humane, more personal aspects of your teaching syllabus.

When personal incidents occur, your response is required. Until you come to grips with events such as the ones described here, the more formal parts of the curriculum may need to be laid aside, because individuals or groups of students can become completely absorbed in the incidents instead. The vignettes in this section are worthy of consideration because you can transfer suggested solutions for them to other occasions in your classroom. I am speaking not only about a child who has been absent from school for an extended period of time, but about any child who becomes confused about what is expected of her. I am speaking not only about telling relevant family stories, but about recognizing the teacher as a living, breathing human being in the classroom, a person with hopes and dreams similar to those held by every student in the classroom. These vignettes should help as you develop your own strategies for a rich, responsive curriculum within the more formal, written one you are expected to teach.

"I don't know what we're doing!"

How to help children after extended absence.

- **Pair students**
- **Clarify objectives**
- **Jump-start instruction**
- **Use your plan book**
- **Provide extra attention**
- **Work with parents**
- **Communicate with other teachers**
- **Invite sharing**

Setting the Scene

School and community: Coleytown Elementary School, Westport, Connecticut, a suburban school district

Teacher: Mara Schwartz

Description: Second-grade reading workshop; I visited this classroom weekly to gather research material for this book

The Story

Seven-year-olds are seated comfortably in the meeting area, some on the couch, others on the carpeted floor. Mara has been teaching reading comprehension strategies to the class over an extended time. Today she continues to talk about how good readers ask themselves questions and make predictions as they read. She gives clear instructions for the workshop time, and children are ready to work. As they leave the meeting area for their tables, where **book baskets** are placed for the reading period, Tracy blurts out, "I don't know what we're doing!"

There is a good reason for her discomfort. She was absent from school the previous week because her family returned late from the holiday break. This means she was actually away from school a total of three weeks: two for the vacation plus an extra one with her family. For a second grader, being away from school this long can be colossal. Tracy feels lost and seems panicked.

Mara reaches out to give her physical and mental support. She puts her arm around Tracy to comfort her and says, "Why don't you work with Pat and ask her to help you? If you still have questions, I'll be right here." Pat is a special friend of Tracy's and they do well solving problems together. Tracy and Pat move to their table. Mara hovers nearby to monitor the situation. She wants to be sure that Tracy is going to be comfortable with the assignment. The girls get out their notebooks because, in the minilessons, Mara has suggested that some readers use their writer's notebook for jottings, that way everything is in one place. "You can hold your thinking if you write it down," Mara has explained.

Pat and Tracy remove their books from the book basket and discuss where to begin reading. Tracy had the book with her on the trip, so they are at approximately the same place. It is easy for them to agree on a common starting place. They begin to read *The Boxcar Children* (Warner 1977). After a while Pat suggests they stop to talk things over. She asks Tracy if she has any questions about what is happening. They talk and agree on a question they both have. Each child writes it down in her notebook. "Do you answer your question?" Tracy asks, unsure about what to do next.

"Yes, we need to write what we think is going to happen," Pat replies. "Make a prediction now." Tracy seems to relax and feel more comfortable as she slowly becomes integrated back into her classroom.

Story Background

School attendance is an important issue. Unfortunately, there are many times when children are absent. When ill, children belong at home. They cannot absorb what is going on when they don't feel well. However, family vacations are a different matter that can present serious problems. No teacher would like to deny a child quality family time, but no family should deny a child the opportunity of being at school. Children need to be in the classroom each day to maintain continuity and the pattern of lessons you so carefully plan. Assignments you prepare ahead of time for a child taking a trip cannot genuinely substitute for a child's physical presence in class.

Tracy had a wonderful time with her family, but it seems unlikely that the trip needed to extend beyond the holiday break. At the same time, schools and teachers can do little about such absences except provide the needed support when the student returns. Tracy was understandably insecure, perhaps even a bit frightened, when she returned to school and discovered that her class was doing different work that she didn't quite understand.

52

*"I don't know
what we're
doing!"*

Teaching Strategies

Tracy deserves a lot of credit for speaking up and letting everyone know she needed help. Another child might quietly look like he was complying with the teacher's instructions even though he really didn't know what was expected of him. What can you do to help a child who has had an extended absence from school? Let's consider some options.

Pair Students

Mara handled the situation skillfully when she asked Tracy to work with a strong student, a good friend, who could demonstrate what the class had been doing and help Tracy past this hurdle. Mara stayed close until she saw that the two girls were moving along with their work. Handing the responsibility over to the students is a good strategy if they have been groomed throughout the year to shoulder challenges like this and you know you can count on them to fulfill such challenges conscientiously. Pairing students is an excellent way to reinforce learning. In this situation, Pat had the opportunity to practice her own learning as she taught someone else what to do. Tracy had the comfort of working with a good friend.

Clarify Objectives

Peer support needs to be structured and modeled carefully. From the early days of the school year, you model individual support as you listen to and coach children during reading and writing conferences. At the same time, you can teach students to work with their peers and give them opportunities to practice the conference model you demonstrate. You also help them know what to do when you begin a minilesson with a clear statement of what is going to be accomplished and why it is to be done.

You can tell everyone, "Today we will work on asking questions and making predictions as we read. This is what good readers do because it helps them better understand what they are reading." Reviewing an assignment after the minilesson makes your instruction more explicit. You may want to ask children what they will do first, second, and so forth. The wrap-up or review of a lesson at the end of the work period carves another notch in this stick.

Students need to become fully aware of the objectives on which they've been working. At the end of the lesson you can reiterate, "Today you worked on your skills for making predictions as you read so that you will learn to be better readers. It is important to think about and understand what you read, so asking yourself questions while you are reading is important."

Jump-start Instruction

There are two kinds of individualized teaching possible in a situation such as this where a child needs to be brought up to speed as she returns to the classroom. The first is the kind Mara used—asking another student to help the child who is confused. But you may employ a different strategy. You may wish to take the child aside and instruct her individually. Whether or not you do this will depend on what the other children are doing, what the confusion is about, the particular child who needs help, and if you know you can rely on another student to assist. In any case, your goal is to jump-start a student who has been absent so he can begin to practice the new strategy and feel comfortable with it. Tracy and Pat were capable students who worked well together. With another kind of child you may decide to give individual instruction and support so the student can begin to catch up. This instruction could continue the following day and the one after that. Tracy's confusion might have been exaggerated because this happened at the beginning of the first morning she was back in school. She may only have needed to become immersed in the class again after her absence to feel more comfortable. Another type of child might need more individualized help, more reassurance, and more practice with a new strategy.

Use Your Plan Book

When you want to help individual students, your plan book will assist you greatly. I always made my own book for planning. I did not order one from a company because it didn't fit my needs. To make my plan book, I laid out seven columns. A narrow column on the left-hand side showed the time of day; five middle columns were designated for the five days of the week; an extra column on the right provided space for notes. The pages were designed to cover two sides of a loose-leaf binder, so the time plus Monday, Tuesday, and Wednesday were on the left side as the notebook lay open, and the remaining columns were opposite on the right. Before I photocopied these pages to make enough pages for each week of the school year, I put in the fixed part of the schedule: math class, reading and writing, science, special subjects, and so on. I made sure there was room to briefly jot down *what* I planned to teach (Figure 7 that is shown in italics). This figure shows you only the left-hand side of the plan book.

Time	Monday 1/4	Tuesday 1/5	Wednesday 1/6
8:45–9:45	Morning meeting Math	Morning meeting Math	Morning meeting Math
10:00–11:15	Reading workshop *Teach prediction strategy* *Use* Owl Moon	Reading workshop *More about prediction* Owl Moon *Check on Phil, Mary, Mark*	Reading workshop *Asking questions* The Relatives Came
11:15–11:30	Read-aloud The Relatives Came	Read-aloud	Read-aloud
11:30–12:15	Recess and lunch	Recess and lunch *Grade-level meeting— my room*	Recess and lunch
12:15–1:00	Computer	P. E.	Music
1:00–2:00	Writing workshop *Leads*—Owl Moon	Writing workshop *Leads*—The Relatives Came	Writing workshop *Demonstrate leads with Jen's piece on overhead*
2:00–3:00	Science *Introduce season changes* Read-aloud— My Father's Dragon	Social Studies Read-aloud— My Father's Dragon	Social Studies Read-aloud— My Father's Dragon

FIGURE 7   Plan book

When all the pages are in your plan notebook, you can write in the special activities you know in advance, such as a field trip, a class visitor, or a school-wide activity. The plan book provides you with a record of what you have done and, therefore, of what you need to do. It also gives you, at a glance, what you may need to help a child get folded back into classroom life after an absence. The plan book is a pivotal part of your teaching.

Provide Extra Attention

When a child returns to school after an absence, short or long, he will need that bit of extra help to get reintegrated into the fabric of the classroom. For some children it is almost as if they are entering the room for the first time. Make sure you greet these children as they come in the door. Give them some attention, such as asking how they are, or if they had a good time on the trip. You can tell them they look nice that day or ask if they have anything special to share—whatever is appropriate. A little bit of loving care goes a long way. And while Tracy expressed her discomfort, some children will not. You will want to check in with a student who has been absent to make sure he is doing well during different activities.

Work with Parents

It is good for children when you help parents adhere to the school schedule as much as possible. If parents ask if it is all right to take their child out of school, be honest about what that means for the child. Giving the child work to take along on a trip isn't the same as being in class. Asking a child to keep a journal, as I used to do, may be a good idea, but parents need to understand that the return to school may present problems for a young child. Parents need to know that it can be difficult for a child to catch up. There may be no assignments that can be replicated to help a child learn the necessary material, and all of us need a certain amount of elapsed time to practice something new that we are attempting to learn.

Communicate with Other Teachers

If a student who has been absent is going to another class the first day back, it will help her adjustment if you communicate with her other teachers. For example, if she is going to a different teacher for math, you can send a note to the math teacher just to remind her that the child has been gone. Or, you can talk with that teacher in the hall before the children enter the building in the morning. Perhaps, the student is going to

56

*"I don't know
what we're
doing!"*

computer or gym class. Here a note would be helpful, too. Many children need your helping hand to ease back into the school setting.

Invite Sharing

In Tracy's case, she was absent for a special family trip. She will feel more at home back in the classroom if you can find a little time for her to talk to classmates briefly about where she has been and what she has done. She may have brought some artifacts to school that she can share, including things she collected during the trip, such as pictures or post cards. Putting Tracy in the limelight for a few minutes will help her feel that she did something important while she was away, and also rewoven into the group as she talks to the class.

Sharing can be a mutual affair. There may be something that happened while Tracy was away that other children wish to share with her. One or two children can talk briefly about what happened the week she was gone. If, for example, you have taught the children a new song to sing while cleaning up the room, Tracy will need a chance to listen and join in as she is able. All of us are more comfortable when we feel included, not excluded, in what a group is doing. You will want to make sure Tracy recaptures her feeling of membership in the group and its rituals.

Conclusion

When your entire class began school in September, you probably did everything you could think of to help everyone adjust to the school setting. If a child is absent for an extended time after several months in school it isn't quite the same, but that child may still feel disoriented when he returns to realize that his classmates have been going on with their activities while he was gone. Whether that student was on vacation or ill, it is both teacherly and kind to spend just those few extra minutes helping that child readjust to the school setting and feel part of the group again.

While you may not like the fact that a family has planned an extended vacation during school days, there is probably nothing you can do about it. If this happens, your job is to make sure the child is tucked safely back into the classroom community after her return. Be sure she knows how glad you are to see her again, and help her ease back in as quickly and easily as possible. She isn't the person who made the travel plans, and you want to be sure she doesn't suffer any consequences for how the adults in her life have designed her days.

"I can't find them anywhere!"

How to help students who mislay or forget things they need in school.

- **Offer quiet, calm assistance**
- **Establish logical consequences**
- **Be consistent**
- **Build in small acts of responsibility**
- **Use sticky notes**
- **Provide substitute material**
- **Develop a verbal checklist**

Setting the Scene

School and community: Greens Farms School, Westport, Connecticut, a suburban school district

Teacher: Nicole Fieschel

Description: Self-contained second-grade classroom; a beginning teacher with whom I worked regularly as a mentor

The Story

There is palpable excitement in the room as children gear up for the next activity. Everyone is scurrying around to gather the things each has prepared for today's culminating experience. The children have worked in groups of four or five. Each group has read and discussed a nonfiction book about extreme weather conditions with their teacher, Nicole Fieschel. After the reading was finished, groups worked on a presentation for the class. Children made illustrations, decided who would say what, and had some time to rehearse. Extreme weather is right here in the classroom as students gather in the meeting area and anticipation builds.

Lee's group read *Hurricanes* (Hopping 1995). They are ready except for Lee, who is in a panic. "I can't find them anywhere!" he shouts, as he tears through the mass of paper in his desk. He is searching for the posters he made to illustrate the stages of a hurricane and feels responsible to his group for presenting them to the class.

57

Jim rushes over to help Lee. They dump everything out of the desk and begin flying through it. "Not this, and not this. It's not here," Lee wails in despair.

Nicole walks calmly across the room. "I'm sure we can find them," she reassures Lee. They both sit down on the floor, and she demonstrates how he can sort through the heap of things methodically. Everyone in the class is now focused on what is happening with Lee. Faces reveal that classmates relate to his frustration. Many have probably been in this boat at least once.

Story Background

By the time children are seven or eight and in second grade, you expect them to be reasonably responsible about the things they need for school. Both parents and teachers have been working to teach them how to do certain basic everyday jobs such as putting away outdoor clothing, picking up their rooms, bringing notices home from school, not leaving a lunch box on the school bus, and keeping some semblance of order with their school work spaces. In many schools children are held responsible for short nightly homework obligations by the time they are in second grade, such as reading every night, doing some math problems and/or reviewing a spelling list.

Lee had voluntarily taken home materials to make posters for his group's presentation, and Nicole was quite certain that she had seen those posters return to the classroom. Actually, you can witness this kind of panic in older children, too. Carl, who was in Kate Miserocchi's fourth-grade classroom, regularly misplaced his math homework. When it was time to go to math class, he often couldn't find it. He was worried because this happened with some frequency, and he expected the math teacher to give him some consequences. One morning, I heard Carl request permission to call his mother to ask her to locate the homework and bring it to school.

Teaching Strategies

What would you do to help Lee or Carl? I know you must have some suggestions, because you probably have had this kind of experience in your own classroom. The following ideas are intended to add to your repertoire. Whatever you decide to do, a bit of humor combined with a light touch will help everyone keep a proper perspective on unfolding events.

Offer Quiet, Calm Assistance

Nicole offered important sotto voce help to Lee. His distress was obvious, and he didn't need negative words from anyone because he was already being pretty hard on himself. Nicole sat down with him and helped him quietly sort through the unbelievable mountain of paper that had fallen to the floor when he tipped his desk to empty it. And sure enough, the illustrations were right there, a bit crumpled but good enough for the presentation. Lee looked ready to cry with relief.

If they had not been in that heap, Nicole would have asked Lee to look in the coat closet and anywhere else they might have been. She could have asked everyone to help him by looking but, considering the high degree of anticipation about the presentations, that may well have let loose more chaos.

When something valued is missing and you suspect that it has been appropriated by a student, you can ask everybody to help search as a sort of game or challenge. "Let's see who can find the marker Jen lost," you can say. When the whole class is looking, the culprit can safely locate the marker or quarter or whatever the object may be and become a hero by producing it. This is a face-saving technique with a win-win ending. If you are certain that the finder is the person who took the valued object, you can speak with him privately at another time. Recovery of the missing item is your primary objective.

Establish Logical Consequences

If Lee had not found his posters, there were several choices for Nicole. She could have postponed the presentation by his group to another day. This could feel like a punishment for his group because the other children were ready. She might let the group take its turn without Lee and ask him to bring the posters to school to show to the class the next day. That would have been a logical consequence for Lee but could dilute the group's presentation and the learning possibilities for the rest of the class. A third option would be to let the group decide what it wanted to do—present with or without Lee that day. Actually, children in the group were already talking about this option as Nicole and Lee searched, and they were coming to consensus in favor of postponement.

Back to Carl, the fourth grader. His missing homework was not found. Carl had a history of being irresponsible about homework, so some logical consequences were probably good medicine. Carl's math teacher asked him to do a few extra problems that night and bring the homework for both nights to her before school began the next day. The consequences were mild, but noticeable. Carl was not allowed to bother his mother to search the house and make a trip to school. His teachers viewed that as more of a punishment for the mother than for the child. Carl could have been kept off the playground at lunch time to do math, but that might also have been inappropriate. If he needed to be outside using his large muscles and having a change of pace, the afternoon hours following such an action might have become painful for everyone.

Be Consistent

Having consistent expectations for each child and carrying them through time after time is crucial when you are trying to help children learn to fulfill responsibilities. The rules need to be the same each day and as consistent as possible for every child. For example, you expect students to complete and bring in their homework. If the family decides to do something special, such as going out to dinner, everyone needs to make certain that time for homework is provided. You can help parents understand your expectations so they are not trying to excuse a child or plan an impossible afternoon and evening that precludes time for completing homework assignments.

Still, consistency needs to be somewhat flexible in the face of true family emergencies. If you excuse a child from homework because of unusual circumstances, then it is a good idea to explain the reason why that works in this situation. Being humane is part of your job, and children can understand exceptions if they realize the rationale behind them.

Build in Small Acts of Responsibility

Children cannot suddenly become responsible for their clothing, their homework, their lunches, and more. They need to learn accountability gradually. It is important that teachers and parents work together to help children undertake age-appropriate responsibilities. If a student has a great deal of trouble with papers, with taking notices home and bringing homework back to school, you want to enlist the help of a parent. You can suggest that parents remind their son or daughter or go over a checklist in the morning before the school bus arrives.

Parents of very young children in nursery school or kindergarten can help by methodically looking for notices in backpacks or by asking about them when the child arrives home. By requesting notes, the parent informs the child that notes are important. Teachers need to be consistent in asking about communications from home early in the school day. This sets up a pattern and helps children remember that they have a note to give the teacher. Slowly, most children learn to be responsible for the communications between home and school. As they do, they begin to develop patterns to remember their homework or whatever else they need to bring back and forth.

Use Sticky Notes

If a child needs extra help to remember something like taking a book home or remembering to get his homework from the math teacher because he came late to school, a sticky note may be useful. You can give an older student the sticky and ask her to write her own reminder to put on her desk. Writing the note herself is kinesthetic reinforcement. With a very young student, you may wish to help with the writing if you think he will be able to read it or remember just because it is there. Before sticky notes I used to tape a paper to the child's desk, but technology has relieved us of that extra effort!

Provide Substitute Material

If a child is frantically searching for anything of which there is an extra copy, she can be given that copy to restore the calm that is needed to proceed with class or to help her get ready to go home. Explain to the child why you are giving her an extra copy and limit the number of times you do this.

I would use this tactic a few times, but not over and over with the same child. If she is given material that she consistently loses, then some other strategy needs to be explored. It may be time to begin working with a parent to slowly increase responsibility at home to help her learn about organization and responsibility.

In Lee's case, of course, there were no substitute materials because he was looking for something he had created. When a child forgets his homework and there is no time in class for him to do it again, you may wish to give him some mild consequences, such as a few extra problems that night. Also, a child who consistently forgets his homework should not do it in school instead of anything else he is responsible for, whether it is attendance at morning meeting or another academic class. It is appropriate for him to do it in school only if he is not missing another activity.

Develop a Verbal Checklist

You can help young children if you have a verbal checklist you go through before dismissal. Does everyone have the notice on the green piece of paper? You can move to the cubbies and search to be sure they have been emptied. Does everyone have all their clothing? You can move to the closet area and take a quick look. Does everyone have his or her lunch box? You glance again. This kind of routine will help children acquire patterns of organization. To accomplish such an auditory checklist, it is important that you leave enough time at the end of the day so that the organizing and packing up can be done calmly. The same is true of arrival. You will want to build in enough time so that every student can respond when you ask them to hang up their clothing, put away things they brought to school, order lunch, and give you any notes they need to share. Everyone needs a settling-in time each morning and a stepping-out time each afternoon.

Conclusion

We have all misplaced things. I have a paper gremlin in my office that misfiles and mislays material I desperately need. A certain amount of this is natural and you know the children who are consistently unable to take responsibility for things. Lee was not one of them, but his desk was so crammed with papers that it was little wonder he couldn't find what he needed. His teacher realized she needed to help him learn to keep a more orderly workspace.

When you have a student who fails to bring homework or other materials to school, it is essential to help as much as possible. If that help means assigning extra work, so be it. You can judge when that is necessary. If it means bringing in the assistance of parents, a phone call or a personal talk is a good idea. Whatever it takes to gently assist that child is what you will want to do.

How you help will not be exactly the same for all children. Each case needs to be judged individually and the appropriate intervention implemented, depending upon that child's developmental level, social skills, and family situation. What we ask of fourth graders will be different from what we expect of first graders. A one-time event should be overlooked. A pattern, however, needs to be modified so that it does not become so ingrained that it is permanent.

Mislaid materials or things left at home occur often enough that you will develop some strategies to help your students without being punitive. You can attempt to do something small that will help the child remember, followed by a bit of escalation when needed. You don't want to be the Wicked Witch of the West, but you do want to help children learn to be accountable in a developmentally appropriate manner. Your consistency resides in the knowledge that you are there to help every child who needs to grow more skillful with organization and responsibility.

"North America? I thought he was in the United States."

How to overcome implicit assumptions with clear, explicit teaching.

- Engage in self-reflection
- Provide explicit teaching
- Give explicit instructions
- Confirm understanding
- Ask colleagues for help

Setting the Scene

Schools and community: Coleytown Elementary School and Greens Farms School, Westport, Connecticut, a suburban setting
Teachers: Julianne Dow, Nicole Fieschel, and Whitney McCarthy
Setting: These stories occurred in first-, second-, and third-grade classrooms that I visited regularly to do research for this book or to act as a mentor for teachers who were new to the Westport staff

The Stories

This section contains several stories that have broad applications because they speak to the same issue: being aware of adult assumptions so you can make your language more precise for the learners in your class. The first vignette happened in a third-grade classroom. It highlights how the language of an author can raise questions in children's minds as you read to them. It shows that there may be words in read-aloud books that need further explanation for students.

Julianne Dow is reading *Grandfather's Journey* (Say 1993) to the class that is gathered at her feet. Children are captivated by the book. As the story moves along, Jim becomes so confused he suddenly bursts out, "North America? I thought he was in the United States!" Jim is bewildered because he doesn't realize that the United States are part of the North American continent.

Julianne asks Jim to raise his question again when the book is finished because, as she explains, she doesn't want to break into the magic

64

"North America? I thought he was in the United States."

created by the text and illustrations. Jim complies, and before students begin their work period, Julianne walks over to the wall map and pulls it down. It is a truly teachable moment. Julianne attempts to explain Allen Say's language—to make it intelligible and explicit for Jim and for other children in the group who may be too timid to express their confusion or too uninformed to even know that they might be confused.

I saw another example of how partial information or misinformation caused uncertainty in Nicole Fieschel's second-grade class. She had written the schedule on the board. It included a notation, as it did every day, about the time for **S.S.R.** or **Sustained Silent Reading**. On this particular day Hattie read the schedule and was puzzled. "Why are those periods there? Periods belong at the end of sentences," she remarked. Hattie's voice indicated that she was both asking and telling. It was fascinating because Hattie had seen *S.S.R.* written like that for months and had probably seen it in first grade as well. But she suddenly noticed the periods and needed to voice her confusion.

Her question presented Nicole with a teaching opportunity because she had assumed that everyone understood why she had written *S.S.R.* with periods. She gave a brief explanation of abbreviations. *St.* stands for *street, U.S.* for the *United States, Mr.* for *mister.* Children began contributing examples they already knew. Nicole did not confuse the children with information about acronyms. That could be left for another time.

The third event took place in Whitney McCarthy's first-grade class. It demonstrates the opposite of implied assumptions—explicit teaching and modeling. Whitney uses wipe-off boards almost every morning to help students with spelling patterns and writing conventions. She demonstrates on her wipe-off board and the children use theirs in response. On this day, she divided the wipe-off board into four parts to make things more clear for students. As she did this, she spoke about what she was doing: "I'm going to divide my board into four parts. First, I draw a line in the middle from side to side." She did this. "Then I draw another line going the other way, from top to bottom." She did this. As they copied on their own boards, she went on to explain why she was doing this, noting how it helped her organize information.

At the conclusion of the reading/writing period, Whitney asked children to share what they had learned as a reader or writer that morning. Amy spoke first. She proudly held up her Weekend News to show everyone that she had divided the picture section into four parts and had drawn the different parts of her weekend, one in each section. "I divided the picture space into four parts like we do on the wipe-off boards," she said. She demonstrated to the class how she used Whitney's strategy as a model for her own behavior. She saw the advantages in Whitney's example and incorporated it into her work.

The second first-grade speaker was Bill: "I copied Michael's name from the schedule." Three cheers for Bill, a special education student. He followed his teacher's advice and tuned into classroom environmental print for help. Michael's name was spelled correctly on Bill's Weekend News. He was beginning to comprehend how to find the information he needed in this print-filled classroom.

Story Background

The first time I remember hearing the term "assumptive teaching" was when I was taking a graduate course, probably in the early 1980s. The term recognizes that we make assumptions in almost everything we do and our actions are based upon these notions. For example, when we drive, we assume that other drivers will turn on their directional signals to indicate they are planning to make a turn. We call the airline to make plane reservations and we trust that we are getting correct and accurate information. We tell a friend something and we assume he heard and integrated what we said. We take for granted that the sun will rise each morning. We say something in class and we assume that students hear what we said and that they understand it as we do. But understanding is based on schema, so there are gradations of comprehension within the class.

Your teaching is grounded in a myriad of personal assumptions that may be perfectly clear to you and obscure to students. You may not even think about or be aware of your assumptions. You have an internal plan but students may be confused unless they understand your reasoning and intentions. Your job is to be as explicit as you know how to be, to be thoughtful about the possible confusions that can arise because of immaturity, lack of knowledge, or not paying attention to what is going on. Have you ever wondered if students failed to understand something but were too embarrassed or shy to seek clarification? In my classroom when questions were raised, I tried to explain in an entirely fresh way, hoping for clearer meaning.

Teaching Strategies

It is not easy for you to crawl inside someone else's skin and anticipate their confusions about your intentions or reasoning for a particular

66

"North America? I thought he was in the United States."

lesson. Nor are you always consciously aware of the assumptions behind your teaching. What can you do if students are not as forthcoming as Jim and don't let you know they are stumbling? Here are a few strategies you can use. You should be able to think of others as you begin to practice making the implied part of your teaching more explicit.

Engage in Self-Reflection

Self-questioning should underlie your practices and anchor them in reason and understanding. This will help you become aware of the implicit basis for the planning and execution of lessons. Have you thought about being more explicit as you teach minilessons and confer with students about reading and writing? Providing yourself with the time for introspection is a good beginning step in this direction. Why are you planning a particular minilesson? How will it help your students? Can you explain the lesson so students will understand it clearly? Can you teach with the transparency needed for children to learn the strategies you lay out and to use them in their own lives? Have you made the objectives clear and reinforced them with a summary at the close of the lesson?

Some teachers keep a notebook or journal in which, among other things, they brainstorm ideas for solving problems. If you are a list maker, creating a list will help you look anew at your assumptions and plans. Sometimes I make a pro-and-con list to play my ideas for different solutions off each other. The act of writing things down helps me think through my ideas and see them in writing, which gives me another chance to reflect carefully.

Provide Explicit Teaching

You will want to be very explicit about directions, environmental print, the reasons for using certain strategies, and so forth. You may want to say, for example:

- "Why did I put the months of the year on this chart to hang in the classroom? Of course, because I thought if you need to spell *February* you can look here. All the charts are in the room to help when you are writing. They will give you ideas and help with spelling." Children need to be told why you are doing things. They will not always use the materials you provide unless or until they are guided toward them.
- "Of course, you know why we are doing choral reading. It is because it will help you remember the poem after we say it aloud

several times. You will be able to enjoy it next month and next year." If provided with reasons for choral reading, besides the pleasure of it, students will participate more actively. Another reason for this activity is to help students with their reading, and this can also be explained.

- "I am asking you to jot down words you don't understand so that we can discuss them after you finish reading. Then you will not interrupt the flow of your reading and you will understand it better." Students need to know how important it is to become fluent readers, which increases their comprehension.

- "After you finish writing, please look at your paper and circle words you think may be misspelled. Then you can try to correct them. Your visual memory will help you recognize words you need to work on." Again, the flow of writing, getting ideas down on paper, is an important first step. Not interrupting this flow with spelling concerns helps young writers with writing fluency. You are definitely not saying that spelling is unimportant; you are saying we'll look at it later.

These are but a few examples of how you can be explicit about what you are thinking as you describe an activity to your students. You have a reason for asking students to do something, and it helps them if you tell why you planned the activity, how they are to carry it out, and how it fits into the broader scheme.

Give Explicit Instructions
Giving your students explicit instructions includes being unambiguous about what they are expected to do or how they are expected to behave, together with the reasons why those things are supposed to happen. You don't ask children to move around the room without crashing into each other just because it isn't quite so much fun. You don't ask children to wash their hands before lunch just because you want them to use up the water and soap. You don't ask students to do their best job with spelling when they write just because you are trying to make their lives more difficult.

Explaining in detail to the class helps them conform to expectations that are appropriate for children their age. Consistency in your expectations and in the work you provide is crucial. You need to give your students reasons, and repeat them more than once, because you know that everyone doesn't hear everything you say. If a child has had a bad morn-

68

*"North
America? I
thought he was in
the United
States."*

ing with his family before coming to school, he will not hear what you are saying. You have to hope that tomorrow will be a more receptive day for him.

Confirm Understanding

After you give directions and are ready to send students toward their individual work, you probably check to make certain everyone understands the directions. You may ask several children to repeat the steps they need to take as they begin to engage in their assigned tasks. You could also ask students to explain *why* they think they are being asked to do specific things. It will help if they understand that you are not assigning busywork. They should know that you carefully think things through and are asking the class to do tasks that you consider worth the time and effort they need to expend. If children are confused about either what they are doing or why they are doing it, then you know that you need to explain in more detail, or in a different way.

Recently there was an article in *The Washington Post* about Alfie Kohn, the educational critic and writer (Mathews 2001). It said, "One day in 1967, a sweet-faced, bespectacled fifth-grader . . . was given a class assignment. No one remembers what it was about, which is sort of the point. The student, Alfie Kohn, neatly headed his paper with his name, the date and an appropriate title: 'Busywork' " (A-10). You certainly don't want to be the teacher known for assigning busywork. You want your students to understand what they are doing and why they are doing it.

Ask Colleagues for Help

If you encounter problems that result from implied assumptions and these problems are difficult to solve, experienced colleagues may be helpful. You are quite alone in the classroom with your students and may have few opportunities for observing or being observed by colleagues. Talking with a trusted peer at lunch or before school in the morning may be a supportive way to help you resolve a problem. Especially when you first enter this complicated profession called teaching, a colleague who listens well and gives sound advice can be invaluable to you. Don't be afraid to talk about things that trouble you. Everyone with any appreciation of what it means to be an educator will have empathy for the complexity of your daily life in the classroom.

Conclusion

You owe it to your students to be as unambiguous as you can be, as clear as a bright, snowy winter day in New England. Simplicity and precision should be part of your talk and behavior. As Chip Wood (1999) tells us, "Because our primary tool is language, this tool needs sharpening from time to time. Paying attention to your use of language in the classroom accomplishes two things. First, it will slow you down. As you pay more attention to what you are saying, you will think more about what you are going to say. This will create more small spaces for your thinking and feeling, and slow the pace of your vocalizing. Second, as your language becomes more precise you will find that students understand you better and respond more quickly to what it is you are asking of them" (229).

If you take Chip Wood's advice, you will no longer imply information to your students and force them to guess or infer your meaning. The child who knows what is expected can make plans to carry out your expectations harmoniously. That student will be in a position to work diligently and learn as best he can while moving through the school day and the school year.

"What books do you read to Bess?"

How to put personal stories to work in your classroom.
- Tell brief and relevant stories
- Encourage parents to tell stories
- Write your stories
- Share your reading preferences
- Be a role model
- Invite visitors

Setting the Scene
School and community: Coleytown Elementary School, Westport, Connecticut, a suburban district
Teachers: Sarah Spencer and Whitney McCarthy
Description: Sarah teaches fourth grade and Whitney teaches first grade in the same school; I visited both regularly to gather information for this book

The Story
Sarah has finished reading aloud and students are making predictions about what's going to happen. They give evidence for their statements with support from the story, *The Oracle Doll* (Dexter 1985). Suddenly the talk changes direction as a child (named Misty) links her comments to a book that her parents read aloud to her when she was younger. Misty then asks Sarah about her daughter, who is in kindergarten: "What books do you read to Bess?"

Sarah tells the class that Bess has a favorite book and wants to hear that story over and over again. As Fox (2001) emphasizes, "it's important, especially with younger children, to repeat the same lively stories over and over again, so book language loses its strangeness and becomes familiar. The language of books sounds different. It looks different. It *is* different" (91). Sarah explains that she would like to enlarge the repertoire of what she reads to expand Bess's horizons and to create new favorites for Bess. She asks the children, many of whom have siblings in kindergarten or first grade, what they would recommend. Titles pour forth, *Goodnight Moon* (Brown 1947), *Chicka Chicka Boom Boom* (Martin and Archambault 1989), and many more. The nine- and ten-year-old readers fondly recall their own favorites and begin to add titles of books they currently read aloud to younger siblings. While it seems like a diversion, this reading discussion is appropriate to what is being studied in class about reading. On chart paper, Sarah begins to make a list of favorite picture books to read aloud so everyone can review or add to it at a later time. This **reference chart** will hang in the classroom.

In a similar vein, children in Whitney McCarthy's first-grade class are preparing to share what they did during a lovely fall weekend. Whitney initiates the conversation by saying that she, her husband, and their two-year-old daughter, Gretchen, visited with her parents and raked leaves. Amy asks what Gretchen did while the grown-ups were raking. "Gretchen has a baby-sized rake and she works with us," Whitney reports. Students are fascinated, and they make comments such as "I never help my parents rake," and "I like to jump in the leaf piles." In telling a story about her two-year-old daughter, Whitney is revealing possible topics for writing Weekend News as she tries to access her students' own memories and stories. At the same time, she is becoming a real person to her students, a person with a life outside of school. One child asks Whitney if she has a picture of Gretchen raking leaves, and Whitney replies that she will when the film in her camera is developed. She promises to bring it to school.

Story Background

In years past, teachers were reluctant to bring their personal lives into the classroom. They did not consider it professional, and they may have felt a need for privacy from parents and children. Things have changed. We are much less formal and are more honest about our family life. Helping students understand something about your busy hours away from school is a way of having a more personal relationship with them.

I remember when I moved to a house in suburban Westchester County, New York, in the late 1950s. The house next door was separated from ours by little more than the width of a paved driveway. In other words, we were physically very close. I had moved from the Midwest, where most neighbors were friendly and welcoming, so I was quite shocked when, the first time I saw Mrs. B., my next-door neighbor, she pronounced in no uncertain terms, "I am the Latin teacher at the high school, and I do not socialize in the community."

72

*"What books do
you read to
Bess?"*

Mrs. B. turned out to be a good neighbor, but she clearly felt her job required her to keep a distance between herself and any possible constituents in the community. She was a private person who did not mingle in the neighborhood, but I think she reflected the way teachers viewed themselves and were viewed at that time. Some teachers may still look at themselves this way and may be careful about what they do in the community, especially if they live and teach in the same place. They may not wish to share personal information at school for fear that it will be abused. Or, perhaps they have not thought of the relevancy of their personal lives to the curriculum they teach.

Teaching Strategies

Students love to hear teachers talk about their youngsters and get very engaged with this talk because of the relevancy to their own lives. Many of them have younger siblings, and all of them have keen memories of themselves at a younger age.

Tell Brief and Relevant Stories

You will find great pleasure in sharing stories with your students when these stories are connected to the work of the classroom. When you talk about reading aloud or engaging in recreational activities with your children or grandchildren, you tap a deep well of possible writing pieces. Your comments will also relate to some of the reading work your students are doing. If you have older children, you will no doubt remember stories from their younger years that students will find significant.

Revealing yourself as a parent and as a family member is an important way to tighten the knot of connection between you and your students. You want them to view you as a real person, not someone who lives in a corner room with large windows at your school but has no other life. There is every reason to share with students briefly significant family events when those events can have an impact on academic work. You will certainly find the ways to do this when you open your mind to the possibilities.

Keep your personal sharing brief and to the point. You will want to be specific about how this is related to class work and how it impacts on the general knowledge of students. When Whitney shared the information about Gretchen, she asked the children if they had also raked leaves that weekend. Then she wondered aloud if any of them were going to write stories about special fall activities they enjoyed. She modeled the writing by beginning her story of Gretchen on chart paper. Similarly, when Sarah asked students for recommendations about books to read to Bess, she found out what they liked to read to their younger sisters and brothers. As she extended the reading talk in a different direction, she explained why it is good to read aloud to siblings.

Encourage Parents to Tell Stories

Stories develop and become part of the family culture as parents recall what children did when they were younger. Family stories provide students with a baseline against which to measure the fiction plots in their reading books. This family culture is also a rich source for writing topics. Some people keep a record of the funny things their children did with language as they were developing their speaking skills. For example, one of my grandsons always talked about the "moom." My husband and I like to use that word because it seems so funny, and it reminds us of the memories of baby-sitting with that grandchild. I am sure many families have such remembrances.

Sometimes parents need encouragement to access information for their children, so you may wish to encourage your students to recall classroom conversations about families at the dinner table. This is a springboard for children to ask their parents for recollections that can be added to the mix. As we know from all the fascinating adult memoirs that are being written, memories are a wonderful source for writing. Remembering earlier times will help students relate to the books they are reading, some of which may be in the memoir genre.

Another source of stories is the tales parents can tell about their own childhood. On Thanksgiving I enjoy the memory of when I was nine years old and accidentally spilled the sweet potatoes in the lap of my older cousin, Jim. Knowing about such stories may help your students relate to their reading or access new writing topics. You can write to parents in your weekly newsletter and ask them to share stories about specific subjects with their daughter or son. The more stories that are in a child's pocket, the more possible writing topics he has to call upon and the more schema he has to relate to his reading.

Write Your Stories

Modeling is very effective. Choose a topic of your own and do some writing about your family to share in class. For example, you may write a series of short vignettes about a young child in your family or about your own childhood. I have a set of stories about my childhood dog that I wrote to share with students, who enjoy hearing them and seeing the dog's photograph. As I use these stories to demonstrate how I enjoy writing, my life becomes more real to them. I wrote the stories with care but without spending an inordinate amount of time, and I have revised them over time with the help of student listeners. They are works in progress—not perfect, by any means—but when students view us as writers we provide a fine example.

Share Your Reading Preferences

It is important for you to share information about your personal reading. Have you read the vignette in this book called "Grown-ups *never* read the same book twice"? In that story I talk about how important it is for children to know the habits of good adult readers, and how we can model for them as they learn to become readers. Sharing your own reading preferences, talking about them, writing about them, speaking about the book club you belong to—these are important classroom acts.

If you have a conversation about a book with a friend, as I did today on the telephone, you can report that briefly to your students. They need to know that adults talk about books and enjoy literary conversations. How else will they know that they should be doing these things?

Be a Role Model

Our lives are not composed only of literary moments, or of events that are directly related to school. It may be important for you to speak about your television-viewing preferences. To possibly introduce a different set of values, when the opportunity arises, I tell children how little television I watch. If they live in a household that has the television set on all day and all evening, it is important for them to know that some people live differently. I tell them the truth: I prefer reading.

Similarly, I may talk about the kinds of movies I like to see if they are talking about that subject. I never choose a movie that is violent, and I share those preferences. Hopefully you will guide them to make good choices as they grow older. I feel it is important for me to deliver a message that could differ from what they hear every day at home or from their peers.

After a vacation, when children are getting ready to share or write about what they did, you will have your own brief contribution to make. They may ask you, but if they don't, you should not be shy about relating a bit about your time away from school. Perhaps you stayed at home and enjoyed the time with your family. Maybe you took an exciting trip or caught up on the things you can't get done when you are working. These things are appropriate sources of conversation. If you engage in mental **rehearsal** about what you are going to share, be sure to tell students how and when you rehearsed and planned your share. Again, you are providing a model for their behavior.

Invite Visitors

When you invite guests to your classroom to share their interesting stories, you provide a new set of anecdotes that may become sources for writing or help children relate to reading or other school subjects. Interesting adults provide fine models for young children, whose minds and hearts are open to new adventures and fresh thinking about their own lives. Perhaps you have a parent who has an especially interesting job or hobby or grew up in another country. You may have a friend who is willing to come for half an hour to talk about her interest, such as cross-country skiing. The goal is to create a variety of experiences upon which children can draw as they read and write.

Conclusion

Students are naturally curious about us. They want to know a bit about what makes us tick, our interests, our family. They want to view us as real people. Telling them about the things we do away from school is totally appropriate. The key is to be succinct and make it relevant.

There is much that happens in our lives that relates to student academic work or to the social problems that develop in class. Humorous stories are always welcome because they lighten the tone in the classroom. You will be the best judge of what is appropriate to share and what is not. Do consider sharing your own Bess and Gretchen stories. You can bring the tip of your personal life into view so that you become a living, breathing individual to the students you live with intimately and intensely for the school year. They will appreciate it, and you will learn to feel comfortable being a person with likes and dislikes, triumphs and troughs to the children in your class.

Literacy Stories   3

Reading

A child's love of and interest in books can begin almost with birth as parents read to their young children and babies start to notice their parents and caregivers reading to themselves. I remember seeing my oldest grandson lie on the floor with his father as he listened to a story. He was perhaps five or six months old. He lay there transfixed, in the crook of his father's arm, and watched the book intently, his eyes scanning the open page. It is never too early to begin. We hope that reading aloud is an important activity in the home of every child.

Mem Fox (2001) writes, "The fire of literacy is created by the emotional sparks between a child, a book, and the person reading. It isn't achieved by the book alone, nor by the child alone, nor by the adult who's reading aloud—it's the relationship winding between all three, bringing them together in easy harmony (10).

You know how critical reading instruction is in the elementary grades. What are your goals for reading instruction after children come to school? From recognizing the first words of environmental print to responding to books in a literature circle, from picture books to chapter books, helping each student become literate is the overarching goal that pervades every moment of every school day. You want to convey your own love of reading to each child in your classroom. You want everyone to love literature the way you do, to seek out literary experiences, and to share that love with friends and family. You wish to convey the excitement of discovering a new book to savor. You want each child to feel a commitment to reading, to learn about carving out personal time for the reading act. You want to teach children to read with increasing comprehension and to teach a rich variety of reading strategies they can use throughout their lives. These are no small tasks.

To do all this means to examine reading practices and break them down into minilessons that are intelligible for young children. In order to assist every learner in your classroom, you will want to teach reading strategies in a variety of ways that accommodate the visual learner, the auditory learner, and the learner who needs kinesthetic reinforcement. I trust that you are accustomed to doing this in all areas of the curriculum.

This section is not intended to be a guidebook into how to teach reading. I leave that to others. But it does contain some vignettes that impact on reading instruction, each in its own way. These stories focus on small moments, but they are central to the teaching of reading. Reading instruction remains all-encompassing as you teach the children in your class to be highly literate and to appreciate all the genres of literature that are available to them.

"Grown-ups *never* read the same book twice."

How to help beginning readers join the literacy club.

- Read aloud
- Encourage parents to model
- Conduct surveys
- Share your reading habits
- Interview
- Graph
- Reread for minilessons

Setting the Scene

School and community: Coleytown Elementary School, Westport, Connecticut, a suburban district

Teacher: Whitney McCarthy

Description: First-grade self-contained class with special education students mainstreamed; I visited weekly to do research for this book

The Story

Early on a Monday morning in May, the class is sitting in a cluster. Whitney, their teacher, sits in a chair next to the chart stand. The materials she needs are close at hand. Morning meeting has just ended and the class is beginning to feel reoriented for the school week. It is time for reading work, so Whitney chooses *The Bird House* by Cynthia Rylant (1998) to read aloud. Earlier in the year she read this book to the class in another context, but she plans to reread it this morning because now the children are studying birds, and their morning assignment includes work in a bird booklet each child is making. As she introduces *The Bird House* and holds it up for all to see, Charles blurts out, "But I thought grown-ups *never* read a book twice."

Whitney, startled by Charles's remark, reacts to it immediately. She turns to me to discuss the comment in front of the children, engaging in a fishbowl activity.

80

*"Grown-ups
never read the
same book twice."*

WHITNEY: Mrs. Fraser, do you think adults ever read the same book
twice?

JANE: Oh! I have a favorite picture book that I often read. It is *The Relatives Came* [Rylant 1985].

The children know this book, so I go on to explain that I use it over and
over in my teaching and marvel at it each time I reread it. I call it my
touchstone book.

The minilesson with *The Bird House* gets under way, and the children are clearly enthralled by the book. They listen with renewed interest. No further comments about rereading are made at this time, but
Whitney and I are both still thinking about Charles's comment. Children
go off to do their work, including the assigned tasks in the bird booklet. As Whitney works with small groups, I move around the room to
confer with individual children working at their seats. Everyone is accustomed to this routine and functions well in this independent work
setting.

Charles's statement shines a spotlight on a topic that interests
Whitney: the habits of adult readers. She knows that how beginning readers view adult readers is extremely important. Charles has also stated
that he doesn't think his mother ever finishes a book. Her guess today is
that many of her students do not often see their parents reading, and
that golden opportunities for modeling may have been overlooked.

Whitney understands that adults can light the pathway toward her
main goal, which is to help the children enjoy books and regularly practice their reading skills. Rereading a book is not the only issue. A love
of reading is the seed she is trying to implant in these children.

The issue seems broader and takes on more importance as Whitney thinks about it. Could it be that the subliminal messages children
receive from parents about reading are as important as their actual observations? Whitney decides to find out what students have witnessed
and what they believe to be true about parental reading habits. She knows
that anything she does in class will help bring the issue to the attention
of the parent community because many children most certainly talk at
home about what they do in school.

Story Background

Young children are like sponges ready to absorb language, body language, and social attitudes that could well set a course for the rest of their
lives. Even if their parents have not given it much thought, one would
hope they have an intuitive feeling about the central role their behavior

plays in both child development and learning. When children enter school, their teachers know that they are role models for students in their widening world. Teachers try to model their love of reading and writing, the excitement of discovery when they learn new things, exemplary interpersonal behavior, and much, much more.

A central charge in those first years of schooling is to teach youngsters to become readers and writers. Frank Smith (1985) has coined a term that describes it all: "the literacy club." He says, "Children can join the literacy club with a single unqualified reciprocal act of affiliation. There are no dues to be paid, no entry standards to be met. A mutual acknowledgment of acceptance into a group of people who use written language is all that is required. Children who join the literacy club take it for granted that they will become like the more experienced members of the club; they are the same kind of people" (124). Underlying these words is the assumption that the modeling of club members is a vitally important set of actions for young children to observe. The models for membership in the literacy club include parents, grandparents, older siblings, caregivers, and teachers—all the older people in a child's world.

Recently, our national leaders brought reading to the attention of the general public by talking about the goal of having every child read at grade level by the end of third grade. But it is more than that. I would set the bar even higher. I hope each student will be grasped by the power of language and of story. Reading is more than an act that keeps a person from mental starvation; it nourishes the soul.

Teachers can safely assume that there is a wide variety of reading habits in the homes of their students. Charles's comments helped propel Whitney to launch a brief class investigation of adult reading habits that brought the variation into sharper focus. She began to reach out to the parent community anew and tried to make parents more aware of the modeling they do or don't do.

I hope that this story will be instructive and give you food for thought about activities that you can introduce to bring parents forward to participate more actively in their children's learning lives. When children learn to recognize literate behavior, even a family trip to a local bookstore can inspire them as they look at the customers reading in the store's comfortable chairs.

Teaching Strategies

At the end of the morning reading period, Whitney asks Jake to give each child a sticky note. The children are naturally curious about why this sticky note is being placed on their desks. They ask Jake, but he doesn't know. Whitney states that the class is going to talk about how grown-ups read. She instructs the children to write on the sticky note any one of the following things:

- What the grown-ups in their house read
- When they read
- Where they read

She further asks them to come to the circle for a discussion when they are done. Children write, then gather in a circle in the meeting area, talking to each other eagerly about what they have written as they wait for the whole class to assemble. The air is charged with excitement. The discussion begins.

JESSE: My mother reads to me at night, and she reads her cookbook in a secret spot.

EMILY: My dad reads at night for himself, at the kitchen table, a book.

JAKE [describing a special book his mother reads at night]: It is a big, thick book. She only reads one page a night. It helps her calm herself down.

JAMIE: We read any appropriate book for our level. We [her family members] read separately and anywhere we like it.

ADAM: My grandpa reads outside on the deck. He reads one book at a time. He doesn't reread that book. When he is done he gives it to my uncle. It has no pictures.

CAROL: My mom reads at night to the kids and reads when I am at piano lessons—a book. [She names two books her mother has read.]

It is clear to us from this discussion that children who speak about their parents reading, even mentioning specific titles, are the very same students who could be viewed as already being members of the literacy club. Several of these children talk about the piles of books their parents have stacked up, often near the bed.

In contrast, the struggling readers in the class are mainly quiet during this discussion. One could think either that their parents are not modeling reading for them or perhaps that they are not yet ready to tune in to parental reading habits. We cannot assume they have no modeling. We've all had the experience of becoming aware of something new and then suddenly it seems to turn up everywhere in our lives. Perhaps after this class discussion, all students will go home to observe what, when, and where their parents are reading. Talking about it at school is an important thing to do.

Some interesting issues have been raised, especially for these first graders who are working so hard to become members of the literacy club. For example, it is clear that Charles is not the only student who is fuzzy about adult reading. Some children know their parents are reading, but they clearly have never discussed reading preferences with them. This brings up a question: What are some ways you can help parents of young children understand the importance of modeling their reading habits? Children need a variety of frequent reading demonstrations. Reading aloud is one model, and silent reading is a completely different one. Reading books, magazines, newspapers, material for work, cookbooks, directions on a food container, travel guides, websites, and much, much more is all a part of being literacy club members.

Read Aloud

Reading aloud is an obvious way to model literacy. The reader demonstrates interest in a book, book choice, phrasing, and pacing, and can read with dramatic voices. As Mem Fox (2001) writes, "Since we know that the repeated reading of a book is an important factor in literacy development, it's a huge bonus when children demand the same story again and again. And they'll make that demand if they like the characters, empathize with the characters, or see themselves in those characters" (132).

At Back-to-School night and in letters home during the year, Whitney spoke about how critical it is to read aloud to first-grade students even after they begin reading themselves. I have strongly stated elsewhere that reading aloud should not end when a student becomes a reader herself (Fraser 1998, Chapter 7). And Jim Trelease (1984) wrote about this with great vehemence: "Readers aren't born, they're made. . . . How does one begin to instill in children the desire to read? That is something I believe we can learn from the man who has broken all records in the desire league" (24). He goes on to discuss how the fast-food chain McDonald's encourages the desire for their product through their logo, the golden arches. In other words, he says, parents and teachers alike should advertise their love of reading. You know you have to praise reading with extra passion these days because television and computers have so much allure for children.

Many parents of children in Whitney's class had remarked to her, "You told me to read to him, so I do." Well and good, but there seems to be more to it than that. Charles's statements brought an important issue in to focus—the subliminal messages integrated by beginning readers both at home and at school. Suddenly it seemed that reading aloud was not enough.

84

*"Grown-ups
never read the
same book twice."*

Encourage Parents to Model

Following Charles's comment and the class discussion, Whitney wrote about adult modeling in her Friday newsletter. She gave parents the context for the discussion. She added words about why she was sharing it at this time, and why adult reading habits need to be clearly visible for youngsters who are striving to join the literacy club. She read her newsletter to the students before sending it home so they knew what she was telling their parents. This alerted them to conversations that would probably take place. She suggested to the children that they might wish to initiate the reading talk.

Whitney held a follow-up discussion in class the next week, inviting children to share the conversations they had with their parents about adult reading habits and preferences. It was a long and interesting discussion because a sensitive topic had been launched. While these activities in Whitney's class resulted from a statement made by a student, this whole chain of events could be initiated by you if you wanted to bring the importance of modeling and literacy talk to the attention of your parent community.

Once a week in this first-grade class, a parent comes to school to read aloud to the children. The book is chosen by the parent and the child together. This read-aloud activity could be pushed further. With parental agreement, the parent and teacher might talk about reading preferences as a fishbowl activity. This could be rehearsed on the telephone or on e-mail so the parent is comfortable with the idea. Adult reading preferences could also be made public by having a fishbowl discussion with another teacher, a teaching assistant, or an administrator who comes to the classroom.

I wonder whether adult conversations about books are often overheard by children. They certainly should be, so it would be helpful to teach parents about fishbowl conversations. You could suggest that they have these dialogues at the dinner table or retell one that took place during the day or at a social event where children were not present.

Conduct Surveys

Whitney decided to do a survey of parental reading likes and dislikes, habits, and comments. The children had been conducting surveys in math class, so this was a natural extension of something they were already doing. The purpose was to educate parents further about the role their reading habits can play in the reading lives of their children, and to stimulate additional parent-child dialogue.

Several days later Whitney announced that she would like to return to the discussion of parental reading. Children were excited at the prospect of doing this. The group definitely wanted to survey their parents. A short discussion ensued concerning what questions should be included on the survey to get the kind of information students found interesting. The following questions were agreed upon:

What is your favorite kind (genre) of book?
What is the book you remember best from when you were a kid?
What is your favorite grown-up book?
What books do you like to read the most to your kids?
When and where do you read to yourself?

When Whitney got the surveys copied and ready to send home, several children requested extras. They wanted to query their caregivers and their grandparents, too. Curiosity had been raised, and they were ready to ski past all the obstacles on the slalom course to the bottom of the hill.

The return of surveys was high, perhaps a reflection of student and parent interest in this topic. A fascinating thing that turned up was that many parents read at night, often in bed, which meant that children did not have the opportunity to witness their reading. One mother, for example, said, "I usually read in bed every night before I go to sleep. I sometimes stay up very late to finish a book." Some parents in this commuting community wrote that they read on the train or in airports. When parents mentioned titles, the most frequently cited ones were bestsellers. The importance of marketing can be seen, but we could also assume that people talk about popular books with their friends or in a book club.

Surveys could be broadened to include questions about library use, book-buying habits, and where books are kept. One parent in Whitney's room talked about having piles of books near her bed. Personally, I don't feel happy unless I have a large collection of unread books that I can draw upon to prevent the well from running dry. It is like keeping extra food in the house in case of snow or for when I don't have time to go marketing. For me a mixture of books satisfies a variety of reading needs.

It would be interesting to discover if families buy books online, if a parent reads more than one book at a time, if the reader prefers fiction or nonfiction, if children have their own library cards, and if students participate in summer reading programs at the public library. This literate

86

*"Grown-ups
never read the
same book twice."*

garden can be planted densely with a wide variety of flowers that bloom in succession.

Share Your Reading Habits

It is appropriate and helpful for teachers to share with children their own preferences and habits about reading and writing. One obvious strategy is to do a **think-aloud** with a book. You can think aloud to model how you were attracted to a particular book. Maybe you read another title by the same author, heard a friend's recommendation, or were intrigued by information on the flyleaf or the back cover. The think-aloud can cover the parts of the book, such as the cover page, the end pages, the table of contents, and the index. You can demonstrate how you read into the book briefly to see whether the language the author uses appeals to you and makes you want to read the book. In Julianne Dow's third-grade classroom, children always request to hear the dedication. She has made them aware of the interesting material contained in dedications and other parts of books.

You can also share information about your reading habits, such as when you read fiction or nonfiction; when you highlight, underline, or write in the margins; how you choose books; and when and where you read at home. Similarly, if you are talking to a writing class, you can discuss your own writing strategies and preferences. It is important for students to see their teacher as a person who enthusiastically participates in the literacy club.

In her book *More than Meets the Eye,* Donna Skolnick (2000) says it beautifully: "Regardless of the curriculum in place in our schools, it is our own belief in the transformational power of reading and writing that carries the day. In order for children to aspire to be accomplished readers and writers, they must spend their days with teachers who are an inspiration" (83).

Interview

If you decide to explore the issue of adult reading in even greater depth, children can interview other adults in the school. Two children could make an appointment to talk with their art teacher, their gym teacher, the school secretary, or the principal. They might interview teachers on a particular grade level and discuss the differences in reading habits they uncover. First-grade children could interview fourth graders and report the results of interviews to the class group for discussion. When an interview is complete, it can be reported and processed by the entire class.

As the class begins to see patterns revealed, they can decide what kind of record can be made to keep in the room.

Graph

Children can take the results of surveys or interviews and graph them. They could find out how many people read magazines, newspapers, fiction, and nonfiction. They may ask who reads for their jobs and who reads for pleasure, or both. They can graph where people read most often—in the living room, in bed, on the train, on airplanes. They could document when people read—while children are in school, at night, when they feel they need to find out something specific. The possibilities are almost without limit.

Reread for Minilessons

On the day Charles declared his beliefs about adult reading habits, Whitney demonstrated her interest in rereading a picture book to provide information for work the children were doing. In this way, she used the book again for a new and different purpose. Because teachers have so many wonderful picture books at their disposal and the curriculum demands march on throughout the year, it is tempting to always use a new book and latch onto an obvious lesson provided by that text. It takes purposeful thinking and planning to use one book again and again. For example, *The Bird House* could be used for several minilessons after it is read for enjoyment. It may be used to discuss the appearance and habits of birds, the craft of writing, the author's topic choice, the characterization and/or setting, and the illustrations, painted by Barry Moser. The class might discuss what the illustrations add to the text, and whether or not they are appropriate for the text. This can help children think about their own illustrating.

In my present work I go to different classes frequently. I have a small group of touchstone texts that I use over and over for minilessons. I hope you will consider finding these books for yourself—the ones you love and can mine for everything they contain. This, in itself, is excellent modeling for students.

Using a picture book more than once can help you plan your minilessons, which should be limited to eight to ten minutes so the children have time to work and explore. It takes skill and careful planning to compress a good lesson into ten minutes. By using a book that has been read before, you can focus the minilesson on a particular part, rereading only that section. Alternately, you can focus on the author's use of a discrete writing technique, such as elaboration. In this way, the time factor is greatly shortened. You will model the skill of rereading for a purpose as you dig deeper into the text of a book.

Conclusion

It is important for students to know about adult reading habits as they strive for membership in the literacy club. The more talk there is about adult reading habits, the more you will help students come to understand and learn from them. It was apparent from Charles's statement and the following discussion on that Monday morning that parental reading could be somewhat mysterious for children in the first grade. If parents do most of their reading out of their children's view, then young children do not benefit from modeling. You may wish to encourage families to engage in reading conversations and set aside time for silent reading or reading clubs at home, not as a substitute for reading aloud but as additional reading activity, perhaps as an antidote to television and computer games.

If you teach in a school where the parents of your students are not readers, your job is different. Perhaps you need to encourage parents first to read aloud with their young children or to listen to their children read the books they borrow and bring home from school. All parents or caregivers need to understand that every reading act is an opportunity for modeling. Reading directions, magazines, signs, labels, and newspapers are all demonstrations. Talking about why parents do or don't like to read is instructive. For teachers who work with a population of families who are essentially not readers, I would like to suggest a look at Eve Bunting's picture book *The Wednesday Surprise* (1989). This is a story about a child who helps her grandmother learn to read.

This story began with Charles's surprise about rereading, and it brought up the importance of modeling reading habits and preferences. If parents are willing to work with you, together you can have a powerful impact on young children's literacy learning. You can bring reading to the foreground by designing surveys, using newsletters, and talking about modeling at Back-to-School Night and at curriculum meetings. You can help parents become aware of the significance of having discussions about reading at the dinner table, in the car driving to school or the grocery store, in the bookstore, or anywhere they seem appropriate. At the same time, you will be sharing your own reading habits with students. The more, the better.

"Chains are too heavy. They wouldn't work with kites."

How to teach poetry and its figurative language.
- **Introduce metaphor**
- **Diversify language**
- **Collect poems**
- **Write and celebrate poetry**
- **Perform choral reading**
- **Sing**

Setting the Scene

School and community: Coleytown Elementary School, Westport, Connecticut, a suburban district

Teacher: Whitney McCarthy

Description: First grade, self-contained with special education students mainstreamed; I visited weekly while doing research for this book

The Story

At the end of March, Whitney McCarthy reads her first-grade class a poem that she has printed on chart paper. She points to each word as she reads so children can follow along. The poem is called "Paper Dragons" by Susan Alton Schmeltz (1983).

A look of puzzlement settles on eager, upturned faces. John questions, "Paper scales?" He doesn't understand. He is thinking about a bathroom scale. Before discussing the language, Whitney rereads the poem aloud. Then she engages in a third reading, with children joining her. Next she asks why the poet wrote *paper scales*, and John continues to wrestle with the language. He speculates that maybe the author thinks kites are like dragons. The scales "might be small and flap around." The class then turns to consider another word in the poem—*chains*:

JEB: Chains are too heavy; they wouldn't work for flying kites.

CATHRYN: No. They would work if they were small.

90

"Chains are too heavy. They wouldn't work with kites."

LEAH: Chains would work if they were small and you wrapped them around the thing you hold onto. [She repeats words from the poem, *fiber chains,* and thinks for a minute.] Fiber is . . . [hesitating] like string. That would work. [She points to the frayed knees of her own jeans.] That's fiber.

The class continues to talk about why a poet would use such unusual language. This question is hard for six-year-olds because they usually are quite literal in their interpretation of language. John states that the author uses unusual language because a poem should be short so you can read more than one poem in a day. Katie remains puzzled, wondering why the poet used these words since kites are not dragons with tails and aren't real.

Tiffany thinks she has the answer: "The head of the kite is the head of a dragon, and the string of the kite is like a dragon's tail."

The conversation continues. Some children are interested in trying to analyze the language of the poem, but it is not certain that many of them understand the metaphorical meanings. They seem to feel that the kite has to look like a dragon. Then it is okay.

Don Graves (1992) tells us, "Metaphors allow us to avoid the clichés of the everyday and see and experience the ordinary afresh" (61). The new insights about "Paper Dragons" are clear for a few of the students, but probably not for most. First graders have difficulty envisioning symbolic language. In their discussion they have used similes, but metaphor is a very difficult level of language usage. This is not to say you should shy away from introducing metaphoric language in first grade or even kindergarten. On the contrary, it is probably never too soon to begin. In the early grades, just saying the words and getting children accustomed to hearing symbolic language is a good idea.

Story Background

Early in my teaching career I had absolutely no idea about how to teach poetry. It seemed as if special knowledge was required to teach it well, if at all. My current impressions are that a feeling of inadequacy about poetry exists in many teachers with whom I work.

In the mid-1980s, I attended an International Reading Association meeting and registered for a workshop taught by some of the luminaries in the world of children's poetry: Lee Bennett Hopkins, X. J. Kennedy, Karla Kuskin, Myra Cohn Livingston, and Charlotte Zolotow. They helped demystify poetry and led me to realize that poetry is important enough to be incorporated into the daily classroom routine, not reserved for a separate unit of study. I suddenly understood how I had neglected poetry and deprived my students of some real enjoyment. As Katie Wood Ray (1999) notes, "Choral readings, performance poems. Large groups, small groups. Playing around with a text to get the sound of it filling our classrooms. These kinds of engagements give students a working knowledge of texts which they can use as they do the closer study of reading like writers" (86).

I began to put poems on charts and to experiment with choral reading. I discovered what fun it is to share poems and have a backlog of memorized poems that children know and can call to mind at unpredictable moments. I realized how poems and songs can sit in our long-term memories to provide a residue of cultural heritage for later recall and enjoyment. I handed out composition books and my students kept poetry journals. In these journals they collected poems they loved and wrote their own poetry throughout the school year. The luminaries would have applauded as poetry helped bind our classroom community together more closely.

"Our lives are surrounded by poems," says Donald Graves (1992). "They come out of the mouths of friends, or of small children, they are inspired by an itch, a symphony, or a repetition of sound, they record the same line spoken again and again by an impatient child or a used car salesman" (2). Many youngsters are brought up with a poetic heritage: Mother Goose, Robert Louis Stevenson, and A. A. Milne. I still remember poems by Dorothy Aldis that I heard as a preschooler. Children know jump-rope rhymes and jingles. Graves adds, "Poetry brings sound and sense together in words and lines, ordering them on the page in such a way that both the writer and the reader get a different view of life" (3).

Young children and poetry do seem to be a natural combination. Many poems are both accessible and concrete for young listeners and readers. The predictability of rhyme helps early readers. When we encounter the astonishment of a poem like "Paper Dragons," with metaphoric language that children must struggle with to grasp its meaning, our job is to support them as they try to unlock its meaning.

Teaching Strategies

Georgia Heard (1999) explains, "One of the joys of metaphor and simile is that it gives us a 'leap.' . . . Metaphor and simile are like windows into other worlds. They help us express our experiences in a new way—a comparison between two essentially unlike worlds" (41). By the time

92

"Chains are too heavy. They wouldn't work with kites."

they reach fourth grade, many children understand the concept of similes and metaphors, though some still need specific explanations when they encounter this kind of language. While many nine-year-olds can recognize and talk about the metaphors they come across in their reading, they still don't employ metaphors in their own writing, whether poetry or prose. In other words, they can talk the talk but cannot yet walk the walk.

Introduce Metaphor

I was working in Deb Bell's fourth-grade classroom at Greens Farms School in Westport. She was a beginning teacher and I was her mentor. She asked me to help with a class study of poetry. One morning I introduced Eve Merriam's poem "How to Eat a Poem" (1967). The poem was printed on a chart for the group to look at as they heard, spoke, and then began to discuss it.

I probed for responses to determine if there was general comprehension. Alyssa said immediately that you didn't really eat a poem, that the eating represented the way one could enjoy poetry. Since she spoke first, I was not certain that everyone in the group had that understanding. Perhaps if I had been more familiar with the students, I would have known not to call on Alyssa first but to let the group grapple with this idea longer. In any case, as they learned this poem and lived with it longer, more students began to grasp its deeper meaning.

Although I did not discuss it during this first encounter, I also chose this poem because it doesn't rhyme. When children write poetry they usually try to rhyme; this is their concept of what poetry is. Roses are red. Because of this, poetry writing can become stilted or trite, even meaningless. After this introduction, Deb and I could later return to Eve Merriam as an example of a poet who does not force rhyme.

Diversify Language

Don Graves (1992) suggests asking students what something is like to move them "into metaphorical territory" (61). If a writer attempts to describe what a concrete observation or thing is like, she will probably employ some symbolic language, either a simile or a metaphor.

Similes are easier than metaphors because them use the word *like* or *as,* and they are closer to the way we usually speak. As the discussion of "Paper Dragons" showed, first graders use similes in their everyday talk. They can learn to use similes in their writing when the device is brought to their attention. They also enjoy discussing homophones, bringing a kind of language play into their lives. In a second-grade classroom I used the Fred Gwynne books *A Chocolate Moose for Dinner* (1976) and *The King Who Rained* (1970) to reinforce the confusing but enjoyable aspects of English. Together with seven-year-olds I explored idioms. Children collected them as they began to write down the idioms we used in classroom conversation: "He was in hot water." "That's par for the course." "She has a bird's appetite." Then students listened for idioms at home and on TV. It was amazing how many they found. We wrote idioms on a large reference chart, and children copied and illustrated each new idiom for their personal idiom books. Soon expressions and idioms began to show up in student writing. Looking at this kind of language is a natural lead into the understanding of metaphor.

Later in the year the same second-grade class went on to discuss metaphors. We looked at both poetry and prose. Our discussions heightened everyone's awareness and students learned to put sticky notes on pages where they found metaphors in their reading. In *Grand Conversations: Literature Groups in Action,* Ralph Peterson and Maryann Eeds (1990) discuss the meaning of symbol and extended metaphor: "Symbols in the world of story function to put the reader in touch with meaning that cannot be stated directly—the extended metaphor of the work. Abstract meanings are made accessible to the mind and heart of the reader through symbols. Symbols exercise an unconscious influence on our interpretations" (44). I learned in teaching reading and writing to seven- and eight-year-olds that children could begin to understand concepts such as metaphor that used to be reserved for older students. They begin to integrate these notions at their own developmental level.

Collect Poems

Earlier I mentioned giving children composition books and encouraging them to collect poems they like. I assume that your classroom is loaded with poetry books and that reading poetry is an everyday occurrence. Either you have poetry books in your own collection or perhaps you use a public library. In our town we are fortunate because the children's department at the public library has a very large collection and we can borrow unlimited numbers of books. Years ago teachers lobbied for and received a special teacher loan period that is double the three weeks allowed to patrons of the regular collection. We can also renew books on the telephone. You may wish to try for similar perks at your public library.

In Deb Bell's class I discovered that children need to learn how to copy poems. The line breaks, white spaces, and punctuation that have been carefully thought through by poets should be respected. They convey the author's intentions as they help us read and understand the poem.

94

"Chains are too heavy. They wouldn't work with kites."

They reinforce the rhythm intended by the author. I observed that children were copying words without looking at line breaks. They needed a minilesson on how to copy a poet's words. The space in the composition books we had given them made this difficult, but they learned to work within the confines of these pages.

Write and Celebrate Poetry

Some students naturally love to write poetry. They enjoy experimenting with language. Occasionally you will see a piece of student prose writing that seems as if it would be more appropriately written as a poem. When I notice this, I suggest to a student that he place slashes between words where he feels the breaks naturally occur. The slashes indicate line breaks before he rewrites his words in poetic form. He can experiment with different ways of constructing the line breaks. Reading poetry helps students conceive of ways to do this and how to think of eliminating unnecessary wordage to make their poems more concise and powerful.

Once in a second-grade classroom, the entire class participated in helping a student decide how to write her poem, particularly where to put the line breaks. I photocopied the words of the poem for several groups of children. Each group worked on the line breaks and later on a performance of the poem for the entire class. When we finished doing this, the author had a much clearer idea of how she wanted to present her poem, and everyone could envision the variety of possibilities.

Writing poetry comes naturally to some children, but others need to do a lot of poetry reading, listening, and speaking before they are ready to try. You can help them understand the wide range of possible topics and the variety of forms that can be used. Many children think of poetry as jingles and Mother Goose, primarily as rhyming. I have already remarked that when children try to rhyme their poems, the result is often stilted and somewhat meaningless. You can broaden their horizons when you present the idea that many poets do not use rhyme. It is not difficult to find non-rhyming poems. I often use poems from *Reflections on a Gift of Watermelon Pickle . . . And Other Modern Verse,* collected by Stephen Dunning, Edward Leuders, and Hugh Smith. You can search poetry anthologies to find non-rhyming poems and put some on chart paper for choral reading to reinforce the suggestion that rhyme is not a requirement for poetry writing.

Children will want to share their poems with classmates. You know the importance of audience. Peers can help with suggestions for revision, and occasionally the entire group can work on a poem, such as assisting with line breaks. A group can help with elaboration and word choice or suggest similes, metaphors, and other poetic language to a budding poet. There are many writers in the classroom to support your writers of poetry.

Many teachers have organized classroom poetry festivals to encourage poetic writing and celebrate it. This kind of celebration can be informal, even spontaneous, just for the class. Or, it can be more formal, with another class or parents in attendance. If it is to be a real celebration, then you may want to think about the inclusion of food, but the most important part of any celebration is the enjoyment of language and appreciation of a writer's achievement.

Perform Choral Reading

Choral reading is important for many reasons. It can help invade the classroom as hanging moss can invade trees in the south. Like the moss, poetry can be delicate and beautiful, adding to our appreciation of language. The choral reading experience reinforces our love and excitement about poetry. Your class can divide into groups, like a musical chorus, with separate parts for different voices. Once you teach children how to read or speak a poem with separate groups and in flexible ways, they will have lots of ideas of their own about how to do it with fresh poems. I would suggest reading a poem through several times as a whole group so that everyone can gain appreciation for the poem by itself. Then you can divide into parts and make it into an informal performance.

In my classroom we always had a group of poems on the chart stand. We concentrated on one for a time until we knew it by heart, but then we returned to poems we loved and looked at them again and again throughout the year. They became good friends and a part of our class repertoire. Some of the poems I chose for the chart stand were topical—they may have dealt with a season or a holiday. Sometimes they were poems students had written or found in their reading. Often they were poems I loved. A rich variety spiced our poetic lives.

Sing

Music is another form of poetry that can play an important part in the classroom. Julianne Dow, a third-grade teacher at Coleytown Elementary School, plays quiet tapes when her children write, and they sing as they are gathering for a meeting. One student plays a gong to punctuate the gathering song. This is a rotating job so that everyone gets to try it.

In some classrooms children sing as they clean up, wash their hands for lunch, or get ready to leave the room. Singing helps everyone focus on the job at hand, and it cuts down on distractions. It brings the group together. Often a class will discover a favorite song they want to sing. It

96

"Chains are too heavy. They wouldn't work with kites."

becomes like a password or a signature for that class as it creates the feeling of belonging to a joyful and loving community.

Conclusion

Poetry is appropriate for all ages. With poetry comes metaphor and simile—new ways to express one's feelings and observations. The poems children memorize as a youngster will probably stay with them throughout their lives. You remember the poetry you learned as a toddler, an elementary school student, and a teenager. I imagine you can still recite the selections from Shakespeare that you memorized in your high school English class as well as the jump-rope jingles you said when you were six or seven years of age.

Poetry provides a lightness of being in class, a different kind of joy and belonging. It is natural for poetry to be a part of everyday life, not something special for the month of May as the school year is running out and you are rushing to cover the curriculum. Integrating poetry and its symbolic language into the everyday life of your classroom helps children view it as an important part of the literate lives they are learning to lead. When you make poetry a daily celebration, you give students a gift for a lifetime.

"I wish he would just get on with it so we can hear what happens next!"

How to pace and evaluate the read-aloud.

- **Minimize interruptions**
- **Pace yourself**
- **Structure the read-aloud**
- **Teach students to take notes**
- **Engage in assessment**

Setting the Scene

School and community: Elementary school in a small city in the New York metropolitan area

Description: Fourth-grade classroom in which I worked as a staff developer for a ten-week period

The Story

The teachers I have had the privilege of working with as a researcher or staff developer, are deeply committed to at least one solid chunk of read-aloud time each school day. Typically they read to students early in the morning to begin the day with a literacy event, right after recess to lower pounding hearts and strident voices, or just before the end of the school day to knit the classroom community together before the rising tension of dismissal. Another common way to use the read-aloud is as a mini-lesson text preceding reading workshop, book club discussions, or the writing workshop.

This story highlights a read-aloud period held prior to literature circle discussions. Several weeks earlier, the teacher, John, had announced that he planned to move the reading from dismissal time to the morning on days when the book clubs convened. At that time, he explained how he would discuss a point from the read-aloud book in his minilesson and ask students to use that same point as the focus for literature circle discussions. His goal was to provide more structure to literature circle

98

*"I wish he would
just get on with it
so we can hear
what happens
next!"*

talk. For example, if a chapter ending left the reader/listener wanting to plunge into the next chapter, students would be expected to discuss chapter endings in the books they were reading, such as:

- Making predictions of what would happen next based on that ending, citing evidence from what they knew about the story so far
- Evaluating the chapter ending, noting if they liked it or not, and why

This model for the read-aloud went smoothly in the beginning. The book club talk appeared more intentional, organized, and thoughtful once a specific focus was modeled in class. But then, as so often happens, a surprise occurred. Students were really pulled into the novel John was reading, *Forest* (Lisle 1993). The author had done such an excellent job of building suspense that children were eagerly awaiting the next installment, and they came to the meeting area with a high level of anticipation. John began with extended teacher talk about a point from the previous reading session. Later, he interrupted his reading frequently to comment or initiate discussion. He was talking more than reading, and as time progressed the body language of students began to indicate impatience and disinterest.

The literature circle discussions that followed went smoothly enough because the children understood how to conduct them, though on this day they had a very limited time for this activity because the read-aloud had stretched out so long. When the book club discussions concluded, a small group of students gathered at the door to leave the classroom for math class. They were talking quietly among themselves as they waited, and two boys were speaking about *Forest*. One expressed utter frustration, commenting, "Does he *have* to talk so much? I wish he would just get on with it so we can hear what happens next!"

Story Background

When teachers build read-aloud into their regular schedule, they usually have a long list of favorite books to read and choose books thoughtfully. They frequently learn to read dramatically in a range of voices designed to engage listeners. They are convinced that they are doing the right thing. And they are.

Just listen to some well-respected writers speak on this subject. Nancie Atwell (1998) says, "Everyone is enthralled by a good read-aloud.

Hearing literature brings it to life and fills the classroom with an author's language. The teacher's voice becomes a bridge for kids, taking them into territories they might never have explored because they don't yet have schemas for a genre, subject, author, or period. Read-alouds point kids toward new options in their choices of books and authors. They show kids how they might approach problems in their own writing. And they provide a communal reading experience in which we enter and love a book together" (144).

Joanne Hindley (1996) tells us, "Gathering together to share a good story builds community and these books become resources for talking about literature. They provide a foundation everyone can have in common" (99).

Katie Wood Ray (1999) says, "As students gather on our carpets to listen to the read-aloud, they bring with them their identities as both readers and writers. . . . Whoever we are most at a particular moment guides what we hear and see and feel, guides how we respond and what we say and do" (69).

But remember, the reader is also a teacher. For this reason, the read-aloud can hold certain perils as the teacher mines the read-aloud for instructional purposes and tries to get the most out of every minute of the school day. This story demonstrates how problems can arise when you put on your teacher hat to share a read-aloud with students. In the name of doing your job, you can diminish the possibilities.

In addition to the reasons mentioned by Nancie Atwell, Joanne Hindley, and Katie Wood Ray, the rationale for read-aloud time includes:

- To examine some aspect of an author's craft
- To relax and have pleasure
- To tie into a social studies or science unit
- To speak to deeply felt concerns of students

Teaching Strategies

The comment "I wish he would just get on with it" shook me to consider the issues that ride along with reading aloud. This nine-year-old's whisper has broad implications because it speaks to the development and pacing of all the lessons you teach. It is a reminder that you need to be self-controlled and aware of distractions that can dampen what you've planned to teach. I leave it to you to generalize this discussion about teacher talk, pacing, and assessment to other curriculum areas.

Minimize Interruptions

You know that when you read aloud you model and instruct just as you bring pleasure and relaxation into the classroom. While you wrap children in the web of story, you give them models of fine writing for their own reading and writing. John was trying to blend the pleasure of listening with instruction. However, if you want to enchant students, enlarge their worlds, provide lessons constructed in spell-binding language, create suspense, and foster their desire to continue listening, then you have to honor those goals and focus on an almost uninterrupted act of reading.

As Fox (2001) tells us, "If we want our children to learn how to read anything—let alone to read more, or to read more diverse or more difficult material—it helps immeasurably if we can give them as much experience of language as possible (84). The instructional moments you plan as the result of a read-aloud must, therefore, honor the language and story created by the author. It would help if you could return to the author's words and reread them aloud when you are ready to teach, not interrupt the magic of first-time listening. But how do you decide when to have conversations about the read-aloud and when to read without interruption? Decisions of this kind can make or break you as a teacher.

Pace Yourself

You need an exquisite sense of pace and timing. You will want to pace your reading so as to capture the audience. If students are engaged in the world of story, you want to make sure that nothing breaks into that universe. Just as you've learned to read dramatically, the pace of the reading greatly influences your listeners. You have gone to the effort of selecting a good book, so you will want to give that book a chance. You want to honor it, as much as possible, without interruptions that break into its intended pace. It becomes important to monitor your audience and continually take its pulse so that you can act on any feedback you receive from your students.

Structure the Read-aloud

It will help if you focus student thinking before you begin to read. For example, ask children to listen for a surprise or startling point you already know will occur. As they anticipate something unexpected, hands will shoot up when the story reaches that point. When their hands go up, you can say, "Remember this point; we will talk about it later." Then continue reading. A brief, punctuated discussion can follow to focus book club activity or whatever other purpose you intend without serious interruption. After practicing this, you can suggest that students silently mark the place in the story where they notice a surprise or begin to make predictions about what will happen to solve a problem the author has created. Again, these predictions can be discussed when the reading is concluded so that talk doesn't interrupt the drumbeat of the story. Then prediction will be the focus of the literature circle discussions.

Another strategy is to alert students to the fact that the class will discuss a specific writing technique at the conclusion of the reading. For example, you can ask children to listen for examples of descriptive language, which becomes the topic for a brief discussion at the end of the read-aloud, followed by book club talk about description in the books students are reading.

Teach Students to Take Notes

You can minimize interruptions by teaching students to take notes about the part of the read-aloud that will be the focal point later. You can demonstrate the note-taking strategy over the course of several days. To begin, as you read you can scribble notes on a chart that consist of a single word or two. Let's say you are teaching character description. You will write words such as *fun-loving, joking,* and *cheerful* on the chart. Students can jot their own notes as you model. I know teachers who ask their students to purchase a small spiral notebook for jobs such as this, or you can give students scrap paper or index cards to use.

When children first begin taking notes, you can coach them by raising your finger when the author describes a character trait so students understand when to jot things down. Sharing notes will help young learners understand what they are to do. They will have to practice taking notes until they can do this without being distracted from listening.

If students take notes on character description, that topic becomes the focus of the book club talk or reading response work. When the focal point changes to a sense of place and description of the scene, the same supportive teaching can be repeated and practiced. When it moves to unusual language, students can jot down special words they hear. Again, you model so they understand what is expected. Soon you will not need to interrupt the flow of the story as children take notes while they listen to the read-aloud.

Engage in Assessment

How can you avoid the trap that ensnared John? How can you remind yourself that you are walking a tightrope between instruction and enjoyment? First, you can monitor yourself and your students closely. Ask yourself questions such as:

- Am I talking too much?
- What kind of facial and body language am I observing?

You can ask students to evaluate the read-aloud period, whether it is used for a minilesson or for listening only. You can teach them to evaluate on a one-to-four rating scale, four being the top:

- Raise four fingers: This book is terrific. I really like it and am anxiously awaiting the next chapter.
- Raise three fingers: I'm interested.
- Raise two fingers: This is not a great book for me. I'm listening but I don't care much one way or the other.
- Raise one finger: I really don't like it and wish we could abandon the reading of this book.

Students do this quickly once they have practiced, and it is an easy way for you to take the pulse of how things are going. A glance will give you the sense of student reaction. Four choices force students to be deliberate. There is no straddling the middle as there would be with five. You will discover many other ways to use this one-to-four rating for student self-assessment and the evaluation of activities. Of course, you already know not to overdo this rating, because then it will become meaningless.

Another way to involve students is to include a short, snappy evaluative session of perhaps three minutes at the end of a read-aloud period. This could be done as frequently as it seems useful. Invite students to critique the book or your reading. It may involve a discussion, or students could write you a short note. Questions for two sessions might be as follows:

1. Tell if you like this book. Why or why not?
2. Talk about the pace of the reading. Would you prefer it was faster or slower? Tell why.

If you plan a discussion, ask students to take a minute before the group gathers to jot down their opinions. They can use scrap paper or the same small spiral notebook as the one for note taking. Jotting first prepares each child to come to a brief discussion ready to contribute his own thoughts.

Conclusion

Learning to evaluate yourself, your pacing, and the lessons you plan is an important act at the center of everything you do in the classroom. You want to keep students engaged, sometimes on the edge of their seats, awaiting and anticipating the next moment. This is true for the read-aloud, but it is also important for all your daily teaching. You want the classroom to be a healthy combination of comfort and anticipation. The comfort provides the backbone for learning; the anticipation produces the nerves and muscle stretching toward the heart of what you teach. Monitoring your own behavior, together with that of your students, will help keep the body of your teaching vibrant and alive.

"I don't need bookmarks;
I can remember."

How to help students prepare for book talk.

- **Be consistent**
- **Move from abstract to concrete**
- **Offer reminders**
- **Model with think-aloud**
- **Demonstrate note taking**
- **Use sticky notes and bookmarks**
- **Encourage repetition and practice**

Setting the Scene

School and community: Coleytown Elementary School, Westport, Connecticut, a suburban district
Teachers: Kate Miserocchi and Sarah Spencer, who team for reading
Description: Two integrated fourth-grade classes where teachers do team-teaching; I visited weekly to gather research for this book

The Story

This happened in the large fourth-grade group of forty-five students as Sarah Spencer and Kate Miserocchi were teaching strategies to increase the precision of the fourth-grade book club discussions. The book club groups contained a heterogeneous mix of students who came from both classrooms. The teachers were striving to help students grow into the kind of readers who would inquire deeply and conduct detailed conversations about their books, talks in which they were expected to support their statements with evidence from the text.

The book club period begins with a read-aloud: *The Ice Cream Heroes,* by Judy Corbalis (1989). Today the teachers plan to focus student thinking on the use of clues in the text to discover character traits and motivations. Sarah asks students to think about the yetis, or abominable snowmen.

As she gets into the reading, we learn that a shaggy yeti has just given a baby to Henrietta, one of Judy Corbalis's characters. Doug raises his hand to say he believes the yetis care about babies because he doesn't think the yetis would give a baby to someone they thought was going to hurt it. Sarah responds by popping a sticky note at this point in the text. She explains to the class that Doug must be thinking about how the characters might turn out as the story builds up. "Character development is a good basis on which to make predictions about what will happen in the story," she adds.

The boys and girls are instructed to raise their hands if they learn something new about the yetis while Sarah is reading. Hands keep shooting up. Josh remarks that he thinks the yetis just wanted to keep the babies alive. He wonders if yetis eat their young. "Some animals won't eat their food when it is dead," he continues.

"Oskar and Henrietta are talking about the fact that yetis eat people," adds Jen, attempting to extend Josh's thoughts. Sarah pops another sticky note in the book at this point.

The reading continues for approximately ten minutes. When Sarah reaches a good stopping place, she issues her challenge. She asks students to think about the characters in their literature circle books as they read at night and to come prepared to discuss character for the next book club meeting. She instructs them to pay attention to what the author says about a character and to how that character acts, and to consider if they are changing their minds about the character as they read more. Would they want that character for a friend? She states that being prepared to discuss this character, for example, means being able to cite evidence from the text. She suggests they use bookmarks or sticky notes to mark the places where they find that evidence about character development.

Kate begins to discuss how important it is to have strategies to help readers remember their thinking so they can bring it to their book club discussion. She asks children how they do this now. Answers vary:

JIM: I write it down.
KATHRYN: I color-code bookmarks. A red bookmark means it is a very important page. Yellow means it is a page that is of medium importance.
JEFF: I don't think that is so great. I don't need bookmarks. I can remember.
BETH: I like using sticky notes to mark things I want to remember.

Kate shares that she uses sticky notes but has gone another step. She jots a few words on the sticky so she knows the gist of what she has marked when she reviews the stickies along the edge of a book. She leaves them there for later reference.

106

*"I don't need
bookmarks; I can
remember."*

Story Background

Dorothy Watson (1990) tells us, "One of the goals of literature study is
to provide a setting in which students and teachers are secure and comfortable in sharing their intellectual and emotional connections with literature. Students' personal meanings that are created while reading alone
are deepened through the social transaction within a group of learners"
(161). When you organize literature circles or book clubs, you expect to
give your students a goodly amount of both choice and responsibility.
Choice is offered when children choose the books they wish to read and
the group in which they intend to work. Responsibility is expected when
you ask students to decide how much and when to read their books. In
addition, because you have a number of book clubs operating at the same
time in your classroom and obviously cannot be present for each of their
discussions, every group needs to act responsibly. At the same time,
young children need to learn a group of strategies for their book club
discussions, which are actually lifelong reading tactics.

Lucy Calkins (2001) discusses the use of stickies, bookmarks, or
page numbers jotted on charts to help students quickly find sections of
the text that support their claims. She notes, "Almost all children will
insist that they are blessed with perfect memories and can recall any idea
and any textual reference without need to record anything at all. The
truth is, however, that all of us benefit from jotting down our fleeting
impressions so that we can later look back on our own ideas and develop
them, just as we also help our companions in a book talk develop *their*
early impressions into full-fledged theories" (244).

How you structure book club talk and the teaching you do
throughout that work can make a huge difference. Sometimes you cannot do everything or think of every little detail before the book clubs
begin. Then you rely on your observations and reflections while the book
clubs are in process. You will no doubt notice things that need attention
as students are discussing their books.

Teaching Strategies

Some students sound so convinced that their personal strategies will help
them, they could almost talk you out of further modeling. But don't be
fooled; the additional teaching you do will be useful.

Be Consistent

Consistency is such a crucial component of teaching. For instance, when
Sarah issues a challenge to learn about character development on Tues-

day, then she will want to plan for follow-up on Wednesday or Thursday and several times later when the book clubs meet. It is important to circle back to the issue of character in the months ahead after it has been introduced. Sarah and Kate will both monitor the book club discussions to see that students are talking about character and have found a technique to mark the text so they can support their comments in discussion.

Move from Abstract to Concrete

Along with being consistent, you will want to remember to move from the abstract to the concrete in order to make strategies real and useable for your students. While talk is powerful, it can be ethereal for some students. You will want to provide concrete demonstrations of the strategies you are teaching. Many of these fourth graders already use bookmarks and sticky notes, and some already know how to jot down quick notes as reminders for the book discussion. However, these skills should still be monitored and reinforced. As well, younger students have not yet had much opportunity to practice these strategies, and they will require more modeling, coaching, and more time to try them out. Demonstration and repeated practice using bookmarks, sticky notes, and jotting notes will help all your students who are attempting to make these strategies part of their reading response repertoire.

Offer Reminders

If the challenge to look at character development and cite examples takes place on Tuesday but the book club discussions don't take place until Thursday, it would be a good idea to remind students later on Tuesday and again on Wednesday about this assignment. Reminders can take several forms. The easiest for you is a verbal one. However, since not every learner is good at remembering verbal instructions, a written reminder may be helpful. If you have a website that students and parents use, you can post the reminder there. Or, you may have a special place on the chalkboard where you write homework assignments. A third possibility is a special note written and duplicated to take home (see Figure 8).

The website or note has a dual purpose. First, it will remind your students. At the same time, it will inform parents about what is expected. Parents will be able to do a better job of supervising a child's homework if they know what you are asking.

Model with Think-aloud

The following day, as Sarah read to the group, she used the think-aloud strategy. In other words, she verbalized her thoughts for students as she

Reminder: Tonight when you read your book club novel, don't forget to concentrate on

Character Development Clues

Remember:
What do you know about this character?
  Details?
Changing your mind about this character?
What have you noticed about the character?

Use sticky notes or some reminder technique to mark the page you want to cite during discussion.

FIGURE 8   Student reminder

was reading. She told the children she would focus on learning more about the yetis. She reviewed what they already knew about the yetis, did some predicting of her own, asked herself questions about what the author said about these characters, and thought aloud as the author developed information about the characters in the pages she read that day.

In the story, the characters were in an ice cave. "What is going to happen? Why are those yetis putting a leopard skin on that chair?" Sarah asked herself. "What does that mean? What's going to happen next? That chair must be a special place." As she was modeling for her listeners, she was teaching them how to think when they read their own books. She was trying to be explicit as she verbalized exactly what she was thinking. She explained that she would be saying aloud what she might think as she read a book at home, and demonstrating the kind of thinking they should do.

Demonstrate Note Taking

Yet another strategy you can teach students is to take notes. You can distribute index cards or scrap paper, or they can use small spiral notebooks. Together they can practice writing a few words plus page numbers while they read short passages in their books. This may seem old-fashioned and cumbersome now that we have stickies, but it works well for some readers. The kinesthetic act of writing is helpful. You can demonstrate jotting notes on bookmarks that can remain in the book, to help readers find the right place when they need it. If I own a book, I jot notes inside the back cover, together with page numbers so I can revisit parts of the text that I may have underlined or highlighted. If the margins are wide enough, I use those to make notes. Students need demonstrations of all these techniques.

Use Sticky Notes and Bookmarks

Students have already mentioned using sticky notes and bookmarks, but when the group gets together it is good to talk about them again. One of the challenges to you as a teacher is realizing that just because something is talked about once in class, it doesn't mean all the students have heard or understood. Some things must be physically demonstrated and repeated several times. Some things must be written down to help the visual learners. Give your students time to practice using stickies and bookmarks in class before they are asked to do this for homework. Don't rely only on practice at home, when readers are alone and there may be no supervision or accountability. It is better to practice a strategy with the whole class and talk with the whole group about how students carried out this new idea. That way, everyone can hear what others have to say about their experiences.

Encourage Repetition and Practice

Part of your job as an educator is to plan the time for repetition and practice so students have the chance to integrate their new learning. Looking at character development for book club discussions, for example, is something that should be done on many occasions. Your job is to observe the students to see how long they need to practice. Do you look for perfect learning on the part of everyone? Of course not. Some students will not be able to accomplish this task at this time. You, or some other teacher, will need to return to the inspection of character later. This is why our curriculum spirals throughout the grades. During their school experience, learners integrate concepts at different times and in a variety of ways. The strategies of marking text and quoting from text are ones that need to be repeated over and over. A student may be able to demonstrate from the text on one level or on one topic (character, descriptive language, setting, etc.) but not on others. You need to keep plugging away on these skills, just as children do when they first learn to ride a bike or integrate dance routines.

Conclusion

You may be working with young children who are just beginning to learn the strategy to cite the details of what they have read. You are preparing them for the time when they will be self-reliant, the time when control is shifted completely from teacher to student. Carol Porter (1990) talks about eighth graders who participated in student-created literature units: "Initially all of the students . . . had been skeptical about a curriculum that broke from tradition, but enthusiasm took over as they began to make curricular decisions to meet their emerging literacy needs. They took responsibility for the expectations they held for themselves and those that the community and teacher held for them" (105).

Students who want to rely on their memories can be led to use more concrete strategies such as sticky notes or bookmarks, taking notes, and so forth. Physical reminders are more reliable than memory in the long run. Practice with these strategies needs to be repeated a good number of times for students to find one that works well for them. There is no one way to prepare for a book club discussion, so what works for today may need to be modified next month. It is important for you to keep demonstrating and keep helping students understand that nothing is carved in stone when it comes to choosing useful strategies. Modification and refinement are a sign of active learning. It probably isn't so long ago that you never heard of sticky notes, and now you may use them every day.

Learners need to be accommodated. They have differing styles and are ready to learn things at variable times. Repeating the use of more than one way to carry out a strategy helps students as they open up to learning new things and trying out something different. You want to give the message that it is fine to try out a new idea and adopt that strategy or discard it if it doesn't work well. Both flexibility and the ability to change are important messages to send. You want to teach your students that an alert, knowledgeable person is always seeking to learn something new in the quest for increased literacy skills.

"But how would we have time for our book club presentations?"

How to make the most of projects and presentations.

- **Tap into a variety of skills and styles**
- **Reflect and integrate**
- **Offer diversity**
- **Provide for everyone**
- **Agree upon a schedule**

Setting the Scene

School and community: Coleytown Elementary School, Westport, Connecticut, a suburban district

Teachers: Sarah Spencer and Kate Miserocchi, who team-teach for reading

Description: Two fourth-grade classes pulled together; I visited weekly to record conversations while researching this book

The Story

Desks have been pushed aside to make room for everyone in the two classes, and students form a large circle on the floor. Sarah and Kate want to discuss with the students the pressure they feel as teachers to find time to do all the reading activities they consider crucial to support the development of fourth graders' literacy skills. They are wondering if anything can be changed or omitted. Present activities include book club work, nonfiction reading comprehension activities, guided reading, independent reading, skill-directed small-group teaching, and read-aloud time. Now new requirements have been added: activities intended to prepare students for standardized testing.

Sarah asks students for their thoughts about what can be done to reorganize reading activities so the new test preparation work can be folded in. The group begins to wrestle with how to find time to do everything. As the conversation proceeds, Lisa suddenly blurts out, "But how

*"But how would
we have time for
our book club
presentations?"*
would we have time for our book club presentations?" A pall falls upon the room, her voice indicating how important she considers these presentations.

Sarah responds. "*Are* projects and presentations that important? I'd like to know why you feel doing them is worthwhile. Tell us what you learn from doing them."

The most frequent response, like a mantra, is that doing projects is fun. Beyond that, there were several thoughtful remarks about the benefits of projects. Here are some of the students' comments:

IAN: Projects show your effort. My father told me he has to do presentations in his job, so it is good practice for giving the presentations that you will have to do when you are a grown-up.
ISABELLA: They give us a chance to talk about our books. The effort [we put in] shows how [much or little] we liked the book.
JAMIE: It is fun to act it out. Doing that seriously pulls you in [to the book].
ADAM: If someone didn't read the book, they would be curious about what you like about it.

The class shows uniform agreement as they go around the circle, except for two children, who pass because they apparently don't want to comment. When Sarah returns to them, one student passes a second time but Jeff, somewhat embarrassed, quietly voices his minority report: "I don't like projects. I like to read books and just talk about them with a small group."

Story Background

Educators are under tremendous pressure for accountability, which is often interpreted as helping students achieve goals that the public is certain can be measured numerically by standardized tests. The historic factory model of product inspection that has traditionally been applied to education seems to be increasing in favor as the way to bring about success. If schools could only improve their models of production, the thinking goes, they would do a better job of educating for tomorrow's global marketplace.

Arthur Levine, president of Teachers College, Columbia University, in an OP-ED piece in the *New York Times* on December 22, 2000, wrote, "Our school system was created for an industrial society and resembles an assembly line. Students are educated by age, in batches of 25 to 30. They study for common periods of time, and after completing a specified number of courses, they are awarded diplomas. It is a notion of education dictated by seat time. Teaching is the activity that occurs during the time when students are in their chairs" (A-33). At the end of the article, he states, "The largest mistake we can make is to cling unquestioningly to the existing model of schooling. We need a new vision of education—one that recognizes the unique way every student learns."

One of the conversations I have heard, from the university to the local level, centers around the perception of how much school time is devoted to nonacademic tasks, away from seat time. Projects and presentations done in response to reading are included in an imagined time away from academic tasks. I heard one prominent educator say, "Well, adults don't do projects after they finish a book, do they? Then why should we ask children to do them?" And as the pressure increases for test preparation and its reflected image—acceptable scores—this conversation tends to gain even more currency.

Teaching Strategies

Lisa's remark led naturally into a conversation that reinforced the beliefs Sarah and Kate had about doing presentations as a culmination to book club studies. I think you can assume that the statements made in this class would represent a much larger student population; my guess is that this conversation could be replicated over and over in many classrooms. Colleagues in other grade levels and at different schools have commented on the energy that they see when children are given the chance to report on their reading through project-type work. We need to remember the age and developmental level of our students and provide time for them to engage in activities that provide variety to their schooling.

Should we provide time for projects and presentations? My answer is a resounding *yes*, and I relate this question to a larger stage. Should you give kindergarten and first-grade children time to paint and play with blocks? Is it worthwhile to change the pace after hard, focused academic work with singing or a quick game? Absolutely. Students need diversity and pleasure in their learning experiences—time to work in groups, to recapture their reading with posters and plays in their middle elementary years. The only caveat is that these activities should have a specific, reasonable time limit to them.

Tap into a Variety of Skills and Styles

Presentations and projects tap into different skills and talents from the everyday work of the classroom. Many children do not have time to play imaginatively at home, to draw, to fashion family newspapers, to create plays. To sketch the extremes, they may be home alone watching TV or busy doing after-school activities. They desperately need to tap into their imagination and creativity to prepare them for an adult world where these skills are highly prized.

When a book club group gets together to discuss a presentation to the class, it calls upon all the cooperative skills the members have. How this work will look needs to be taught, modeled, and guided by the teacher, because students must work with each other in new and different ways. Students should decide how to present the book to the class—a puppet show, a poster, a short dramatization—and carry that work to fruition. The project requires doing jobs that are different from other class work. They may draw, write letters, organize, rehearse, and gather and keep track of materials. These tasks provide children with opportunities to improve on other strengths. They need to listen to peers, help members in their group, and meet deadlines. The audience benefits when it learns about new books to read, views unique project ideas, and sees their peers in different ways. Auditory learners have an opportunity to hear about books, and visual learners have a chance to view what other students have created to communicate their ideas.

Reflect and Integrate
Children need breaks and a change of pace, those spaces we can create among the pressures of a tightly packed school day. As an adult, I may choose to vary my day by working in the garden, planning a meal for friends, reading a good book, or participating in an aerobics class. Variety give us time to regroup, rethink, and revise. Projects afford students the time to rethink their reading, try out different skills, and think about what they will do differently or the same when they begin the next book, either in a book club or independently. And, a project helps make the book memorable.

Offer Diversity
Creating projects and presentations provides diversity in the classroom. Nine- and ten-year-olds do a great deal of reading, writing, thinking, and listening in school, the seat-time activities described by Arthur Levine. Projects offer them a different kind of learning—one in which they can work again in their smaller group, decide upon responsibilities, tap into art and dramatic skills, work within a time frame, and do a public presentation. You see the energy they put into projects because they enjoy the change of pace. If students spend two to three weeks reading a book and

discussing it in their book club, and then quickly move along to a new title, they don't have time to integrate and savor that initial book. A project gives them the opportunity to step back, choose an important episode, create a piece of dialogue, or summarize a book before they present their learning to peers. This gives students unique ways to learn from their reading.

Provide for Everyone

Jeff had the courage to give his minority report, maintaining that he likes to work in a smaller group of friends. There will often be children who feel this way. Maybe he isn't confident enough to go public in the way presentations demand. How could you accommodate Jeff? You need to pay special attention to him, to make sure his group helps him feel comfortable. You need to help him find jobs that will tap into his strengths and make him feel he is an integral part of what is going on. You don't want Jeff to be a source of trouble, or sit passively and disengaged. Perhaps he would feel comfortable if he could:

- Search for quotes to put on a poster
- Telephone group members at night to make sure everything is in school the next day
- Create or organize an informal backdrop for a skit or play
- Organize simple costumes (hats, scarves, etc.)

Agree upon a Schedule

The schedule for presentations should be discussed in class. It is important for students to agree on and adhere to a compact schedule so that the projects don't take over the reading period for too long a time. I would suggest a possible schedule as follows:

- One class period to organize and make basic decisions, such as format
- Two to three periods to produce and/or rehearse
- Two periods for presentations

This schedule means that presentations could be accomplished in one week, perhaps spilling over into the second week by using only one additional reading time. If one or two groups are ready earlier, they can present to the class as a change of pace while others are still discussing books or projects. Presentations could also be given in small time slots that are already available in your timetable, such as the fifteen minutes before lunch or just before dismissal. Flexible scheduling will save class time.

Conclusion

Projects are a more playful way for students to respond to reading and for you to vary classroom activities. I hope you won't abandon or overlook presentations and projects in the name of accountability or saving time to try to stuff more curriculum or more facts into your students. They are not pigs to fatten, but readers and writers to teach and enrich. You will wish to tap into the vast variety of strengths that reside in all learners, the ones who read well, the ones who write well, the artistic children, the students who are good at organizing and helping their peers stay on task, and the children who love to dramatize their lives and create skits or plays. In offering the opportunity to do projects, you help students learn more about themselves, including their own strengths and weaknesses.

How much time you devote to projects will depend on the group, other curriculum demands, and your schedule. They can be done in school and presented in class without allowing them to take over the life of the class. Personally, I don't think they should be assigned for homework. If you value projects, be willing to devote class time to teach, model, supervise, and carry them to fruition. They do need carefully spelled out expectations and time limits. Because projects and presentations tap into different modalities, they help diversify the educational opportunities available to children.

Writing

Many teachers find that writing is the area in which is it easiest to begin unwrapping the curriculum layers to reveal the gifts inside—choice, responsibility, focused minilessons, extended practice, and writing conferences. However, becoming a sophisticated practitioner of the writing workshop takes thought, practice, and revision of your teaching strategies. There is an extensive support system to assist you: a vast variety of children's literature and many excellent professional books about the teaching of writing.

After I learned to be a writing workshop teacher in the 1980s, I found that I could envision diversifying my teaching in other curriculum areas, modeled on the workshop style. I discovered that the principles of writing workshop worked equally well in reading, math, social studies, and science. Once you unleash the idea of choice in writing, for example, it is difficult not to acknowledge its value in reading. Once you hand over to children the responsibility for decision making in writing, you cannot be the sole decision maker for other areas of the curriculum. When you devote class time to student practice and discovery, you see the power in this. After you witness the great value in discussions and sharing, you want to encourage those same talks about math and science. In other words, the great strengths you learn in one curriculum area are equally powerful throughout the school day.

There are, of course, still issues remaining to be resolved in the writing workshop that I uncovered as I was doing the research for this book. No matter how well you have your class organized for writing, new questions arise. This is what makes this teaching so exciting. Where is the line to be drawn between student choice and responsibility and our obligations to teach, share, and guide? The Board of Education is paying your salary with the expectation that you will be the giant in that classroom, the one who walks with huge steps. It is the hows and whys of your enormous role that can make the difference. You are expected to teach students to become literate individuals who have a zest for further learning. You are expected to help your students become socialized so they can learn to be productive community members. You are expected, and you expect, to pass the torch, to raise their sights, and to inspire them to love literature and be knowledgeable about how to craft their writing. The principles of the writing workshop—choice, responsibility, time, minilessons, practice, conferring, and sharing—all contribute to these lofty—but very attainable—goals.

"You must have been embarrassed."

How to help students overcome resistance to revision of their writing.

- **Move toward revision**
- **Develop minilessons**

Setting the Scene

School and community: Coleytown Elementary School, Westport, Connecticut, a suburban district

Teacher: Karen Wrobel

Description: I visited this second-grade classroom regularly as a mentor to Karen, who was a beginning teacher

The Story

Twenty-four second graders gather in the hallway-like extension of Karen's classroom, which, being a former office, doesn't have the usual boxy shape. Some sit with pillows behind their backs for extra comfort. Their eager faces are turned toward me as I begin my minilesson about revision. I tell a personal story.

I relate how I recently completed a manuscript and mailed it to my editor, Lois Bridges. "Phew," I thought. "This is a milestone." (Then my voice turns a bit dramatic as I continue.) Lois, a conscientious and helpful person, sent me an email a few days after she received the package.

"Jane," she wrote, "I am sending the pages back to you." She went on to explain that there was not a lot to do, but some "tickling in a few places to make it even better."

Oops. I recall for the children how surprised I was. I had thought I was finished. I had experienced that "I'm done" feeling only a week ago and suddenly it had vanished. Until the manuscript arrived back in my hands, I was even a bit apprehensive. What could she want me to do?

Gina's hand shoots up, an eager and knowing look on her face. Her dark brown eyes flash as she tells everyone, "I bet I know how you felt. You must have been embarrassed."

Gina's words are the genesis of this book. At first I was startled and surprised, even taken aback by what she said. Later, as I reflected on her words, I realized that I had never considered embarrassment as a possible source of the reluctance on the part of students to engage in the revision process. Stubbornness, perhaps. Immaturity, maybe. Inability to understand, possibly. But embarrassment? That spoke to the possibility that when you ask children to revise you may be, in some cases, attacking the bedrock on which they stand.

After Gina shared what was, I came to realize, her developmentally appropriate thinking, I needed time to reflect in order to crawl inside her statement and realize how pertinent it was to the concept of revision that I was planning to teach this class and their teacher. I had been assuming that if I could overcome what I call the "I'm done" syndrome and make revision logical and fun, children would stand ready to engage in this process because they would want to make their writing better. I was asking them to demonstrate facility with craft. In doing so, I was attempting to teach the writer, not the writing.

Gina raised the specter that in asking children to revise, I might be saying to some of them that they did not measure up to my expectations. I would never want children to feel that way. Did they think that once drafted, their pieces were really done? Was their understanding of the process so limited that they didn't know that writers revise again and again, or was this a developmental issue? If it was developmental, perhaps some students in the class were ready to work on revision and others were not. Again, Gina's comment was so earth-shaking for me because I had never thought of embarrassment as a possibility for the resistance I felt.

Lucy Calkins ([1986] 1994) writes, "For me, revision does not mean repairing a draft; it means using the writing I have already done to help me see more, feel more, think more, learn more" (39). She also tells us, "When I draft and revise a text, what is going on inside my head can be likened to a taffy pull. Different versions of my text—some written and some only sensed—exist simultaneously. Different ideas, voices, and forms (some written and some only imagined) interact" (129). The question becomes, can you help children see the revision process this way? This is sophisticated stuff for young children, but there must be ways you can communicate these concepts to the students in your class.

Story Background

In Wondrous Words, Katie Wood Ray (1999) recalls the past for us: "in writing so many of us remember assessment as something aimed at putting us squarely in our place, something that would show us all we didn't do and didn't know" (292). Today, the red pen stays inside the desk as we work alongside students, in the belief that we can help them become better writers by teaching them to envision different possibilities. We confer with them individually, endeavor to understand their intentions, and consider their skills before we make any suggestions about revision. As Ray notes, "Our response can be one of helpfulness" (292). We do it with care, considering everything we know about the writer, including her developmental level and emotional needs.

Donald Graves (1994) writes, "I seldom encourage very young children (kindergarten, first grade) to revise" (235). Some young children are ready to correct spelling errors, and, when they are reminded, most first-grade students will edit so there are capital letters at the beginning of sentences and periods at the end. Editing tasks seem acceptable to many young learners, but revision of text is another matter. Revision is the more difficult act, and that is what is being considered in this story.

Webster's Ninth New Collegiate Dictionary (1983) says *revise* means "to correct or improve, to make a new, amended, improved or up-to-date version" (1010). Revision requires a willingness to look at your own writing in new and fresh ways, to be experimental and open-minded. Writers need a variety of experiences and schema at their fingertips to be able to envision revision. It may mean moving text around, rewriting, changing words and phrases, adding and/or deleting text, and the many other strategies writers employ from draft to draft as they struggle to improve a written piece. I don't think children are psychologically able to revise until they have grown to the point where they can be self-critical, and this requires both confidence and a degree of maturity.

I often encounter that prevalent, almost contagious, "I'm done" attitude. It announces that the writer or reader or math student is done and doesn't want to be asked to look again at the work. "I like it this way," third grader Sam told me the other day with finality as he shut down. This is discouraging when we know from their spoken language that students are capable of more eloquence. The children in my second-grade class were familiar with good literature. They had excellent models in published authors such as Cynthia Rylant, Jane Yolen, and Bill Martin Jr. They could talk about the craft of writing, but when it came to their own revisions, I was often unable to break through the wall they had constructed around themselves, the wall that said to me, "Don't try to breach me because I am impervious." What can be done about this?

You probably have seen pieces of writing that have obviously been rewritten or guided so closely by a teacher that you know they are not really the words of a child. This is *not* what you want to do. But, you would love to see children taking down that wall, brick by brick, as they learn to view their work with a more critical eye. You would like to see them use accomplished writers as their guides, as leaders they can follow with their eyes, hearts, and minds open to new visions. You want to have an impact on these writers as you point the way toward finer crafting.

Teaching Strategies

As Gina made her pronouncement, I asked myself how I could help children re-envision their writing without embarrassing them or having them feel that they had let me down. I then aimed to let the children in Karen's class know that revision is fun, that playing with words and thoughts is a challenge to be enjoyed, and that revision is a skill to be practiced, like shooting hoops.

Some children may need reassurance. In particular, they may need to hear that you know they have done their utmost. After that, your job is to help them understand more about the work of writing. You can accurately describe your own process or that of writers you know. This was one of the first principles I learned about teaching writing workshop more than twenty years ago.

Carl Anderson's book *How's It Going?* (2000) contains a section he titles "What Do We Teach Students Who Are Done?" He writes, "Many students, however, tell us they're done as soon as they've finished their drafts. . . . It's these students especially who usually need our help to learn how to edit and revise. When I confer with these students, I have a conversation with them about writing work they *could* do, and then I teach them something about that work. To get this conversation going I take a look at the student's writing and tell him what the piece tells me about his strengths as a writer, and what the piece tells me he needs to learn to grow as a writer" (74).

Lucy Calkins ([1986] 1994) writes, "Because they often do not turn around to rethink, these children tend not to understand that the purpose of revision is not to correct but to discover" (130). If revision is about charting a new course, then you are not telling children they didn't meet your expectations. Instead, you are encouraging them to be adventurers, to walk down new paths. Calkins adds, "If we can help our students anticipate revision, then we can help them take risks as writers" (208).

Move Toward Revision

After Gina's comment, I needed to get the class moving in the direction of revision. I reassured students that Karen and I knew that they had worked hard and done their best as they drafted their pieces. Now they were going to be real writers. First, we asked them to choose a favorite piece that they wanted to work on again. Then we asked them to sit alongside a partner, an act they were accustomed to, in order to read that piece aloud to their partner. As they read aloud, they were to listen for any place where it didn't sound right—where they thought they could make a change, such as using a different word or phrase or adding words to explain their thoughts more clearly. We said that when they heard these things, they should stop only long enough to mark that place with a pencil. Later they could work on it. We encouraged the partner, or listener, to help the writer by asking questions or making suggestions about things that could be further elaborated when the reading was finished.

I felt the children needed a visible demonstration about how to do this assignment. This minilesson became a maxilesson because I asked for a volunteer. Jim came forward, sat next to me, and read his piece aloud. When he was finished we discussed the writing, and I asked questions that gave him ideas for revision. As the class went to work, I first sat with Jim to talk about how he could actually do the revisions he wanted to make.

It is difficult for writers to see their own work in a critical fashion because they are wedded to their own words and style. When they read aloud and hear their own voices, they can begin viewing the writing as a reader or listener might. I have tried this activity by letting each partner read the writing of the other person, but hearing your own words in your voice is more effective. I felt this was a first, baby step toward revision for this class at this time.

Develop Minilessons

For the next minilesson I explained that though some writers may be embarrassed to receive feedback, I wasn't because I value the suggestions of other writers. No matter how hard I work, my writing can always be improved. I feel lucky to have a peer to help me with my writing. Sometimes I ask my friend Donna Skolnick to read a piece and give me her suggestions. Similarly, when Lois sent the pages back, she was helping me grow as a writer. That is what a teacher is trying to do for a student.

On other days, I brought my manuscript to class. I showed multiple versions to demonstrate that the pages I sent to my editor were ones

I had worked on for months. Because the date appears on the top of my printed drafts, the development of my work is visible. The papers gave concrete evidence of how I print out drafts, use a pen, correct, change, and cross out. I demonstrated how I move text around, insert text, and discard text. I explained how I search for redundant words and repetitions of phrases and cross them out. At times, I had even started all over, discarding what I had written, just as I do in sections of my garden by digging, reworking the soil, and moving plants in the spring. In a series of minilessons, I shared different revision techniques I use:

- *Editing vs. revision.* I used a piece of writing on a chart to make the two different strategies, editing and revision, more concrete for students. I highlighted the differences by using colored markers: red for editing changes and blue for revisions. On two separate days I set students to work on each strategy with a partner. I tried to make this lesson playful, using different-colored pens.
- *Help from peers.* A student writer shared her piece with the class. She asked for questions and comments. I took notes and gave the notes to the writer, instructing her to consider each comment and act on it, if she wished. Older students can take their own notes when engaged in partner or small-group work. Students already know that suggestions are possibilities, not demands. I prefer the language "you could" rather than "you should" when students offer suggestions. I teach the distinction because it helps children know how to make suggestions when they consider the nuances of the two words.
- *Spider legs.* To use this method, students write additions or changes to the writing on strips of paper that are then taped onto the text at the appropriate place. They are folded toward the center when it is time to put the writing away. I demonstrated this by coming to the minilesson with my strips already cut. Then I identified where I wanted to add text, wrote on the strips, and taped them in. Young children love to experiment with this strategy.
- *Conventions.* I used an overhead projector with student writing to demonstrate how to cross out unwanted text and use carets to write in additional words. I taught that a diagonal line through the first letter of a word indicates that a capital should be changed to a lowercase letter, that three small lines under a letter show it should be capitalized, and the backward *P* designates a new paragraph. Children need to learn how to make revision easy.

- *Cut and paste.* Using a piece of student writing for demonstration, I showed students how to user scissors and tape (the low-tech method of moving text without a computer). They enjoy this technique, though they need to learn how to use tape judiciously. This strategy helps children adjust story sequence and elaborate parts of their pieces.
- *Moving blocks of text.* On an overhead projector, I demonstrated how to circle blocks of text and number or letter the circled section, then insert the same number in a different place in the text to show where that part is to be moved. I use capital letters in a circle or roman numerals, but Julianne Dow taught third graders to use symbols they like to make, such as a star or a heart. This method is a good substitute for tape, but it is not quite as concrete for young writers.
- *Better vocabulary.* Children searched for overused words such as *nice, good,* and *stuff,* and replaced them with more descriptive vocabulary that would explain what they meant. They looked in their favorite literature for examples. We began to generate lists of descriptive words and phrases on reference charts to hang in the room. Another day I showed how to search for and underline repetitive words, then find synonyms to substitute. Yet another afternoon we talked about varying dialogue, such as changing the word *said* to *spoke, shouted, mumbled,* or *cried.* We began a list of alternative words for *said* on a reference chart.
- *Description.* With a favorite picture book, Jane Yolen's *Miz Berlin Walks* (1997), I modeled how to write better descriptions of a character or a place. You can model this with a piece of your own writing on a chart or an overhead projector.
- *Leads and endings.* We examined the way authors begin and end their stories. I showed the class the way Mem Fox introduced *Wilfred Gordon McDonald Partridge* (1985) in a simple, punctuated straightforward style, the technique she uses throughout the book. We began a list of alternative ways to write leads and endings. Such a list should be ongoing as literature is introduced and new ideas are discovered.
- *Elaboration.* I modeled elaboration with my own writing, with some student writing, and with *The Relatives Came* (1985). I tried to show how giving enough—but not too much—detail is important for the reader and for the music of the language.
- *Reading like a writer.* In minilessons, we focused on specific structures writers use, such as the circular story structure Cynthia

Rylant uses in *The Relatives Came* (1985), or the poetic, short phrases Jane Yolen uses to bring drama to her *Welcome to the Sea of Sand* (1996). Katie Wood Ray (1999) calls this "intentional and deliberate reading" (15). Students then learned to structure pieces like their favorite authors.

- *From drawing pictures to writing words.* Karen Ernst (1994) writes that "the linking of the visual with the written [gives] students ways to express their uniqueness and their creative thought, thereby widening their abilities to say what they [mean]." (48). We encouraged the children in this second grade to revise and elaborate a drawing they had made. We related these changes to the revision of writing. When they understood how important it was to add detail or color to a picture, they could think of doing the same with their writing.

Beyond the minilessons, you will want to work with individual students, using a technique suggested by Carl Anderson (2000). Look carefully at the writing and focus a revision conference on something the student has done that can be improved. The focus will be a real writing skill that you are teaching this writer, hoping that once a child tries something, she will be able to use it again. In other words, when she learns how to add details, she will think about writing details in another piece of writing. Of course, some children need to practice skills many times before they automatically begin to incorporate them in their repertoire.

In a classroom that is rich with literature, you can read aloud every day and use books as fertile sources for minilessons. Look at style, content, and craft, and talk about these elements of writing with your students. Then help students move beyond the "I'm done" syndrome.

Conclusion

The lesson contained in this story is that we all need to be sensitive to the fact that when asked to revise their writing, some children may feel they are being told that they haven't done a good enough job or haven't worked hard enough. You need to reassure these children so they can learn, over time, that drafts are just that—a way of getting ideas down on paper so they can be used later as a starting point for more sparkling pieces. The children you teach have not yet had experiences in their lives where they need to revise much of anything. The things they do are finished quickly and put aside. Laboring over words and phrases is a new concept for them. You will want to hold their hands as they go through the process of working intensively on a piece of writing to make it the very best they can.

Ralph Fletcher and JoAnn Portalupi (1998) tell us that "there is no Miracle-Gro for growing young writers" (7). You know that you would be selling these writers short, however, if you did not expect them to learn to do more. Children will implement the new ideas you teach if you guide them in a gentle, developmentally appropriate way. In other words, you can respond to them as writers with the kind of helpful suggestions and minilessons that will assist them to improve their writing. You aren't trying to embarrass them or to say that they didn't measure up. Rather, you are telling them that every writer can acquire new ideas, new skills, and take pride in doing their jobs well. This is the greatest gift you can give.

As they work through the revision process, students will begin to understand that this is a messy, time-consuming, sometimes frustrating but often joyful route. We, adults and children alike, write and revise so that readers will be captured by our words.

"I just *don't* know what to write."

How to help students who are out of ideas and frustrated.

- Demonstrate rehearsal
- Introduce guided planning
- Remind at dismissal time
- Compose a parent newsletter
- Create a reference chart
- Generate a personal list
- Reread
- Turn to a partner
- Draw to unlock ideas
- Move on

Setting the Scene

> *School and community: Coleytown Elementary School, Westport, Connecticut, a suburban school district*
> *Teacher: Whitney McCarthy*
> *Description: Self-contained first grade with special education students mainstreamed; I visited regularly to do research for this book*

The Story

The minilesson is over and directions have been given. Children scatter to their desks as Whitney and four children gather on the rug. Whitney will teach reading to small, rotating groups, and the balance of the class will do their assigned work. The boys and girls now sitting on the rug have brought short chapter books with them. When they are settled, Whitney asks, "How did you like the way the author began the part you read yesterday? Did you notice it started with a question?" Hands are raised as students become engaged in their reading work.

I turn to scan the room. Cathy looks extremely frustrated and upset. I move toward her desk, carrying a little chair. "What's up, Cathy?" I inquire. "Can I help you?"

The reply is emphatic and definite. She says I can't help because she doesn't know what to write for her Weekend News. "Nothing happened," she intones. She is staring at the large composition book children use for writing Weekend News. It has space for a picture at the top, and below there are lines divided by a row of dashes to help beginning writers keep their handwriting under control.

Oh dear. She sounds so forlorn and discouraged. I offer suggestions in an attempt to penetrate her armor. I review the weekend with her, but she has dug in her heels and cannot be moved. Since that seems like a dead end, I change tactics. I suggest that we **read the room** and try to think of possibilities. I focus first on the alphabet letters to see if she can associate anything while reviewing them. She tells me, in no uncertain terms, that reading the room has nothing at all to do with her weekend. Perhaps she is right, considering the state she is in. I change tactics again. What about her father? Was he home? Did she do anything with him? Her answer is negative. Her brother? Negative, again.

Now I am the one who is becoming frustrated. Conceivably the best thing to do is leave her alone to see if she can solve her own problem.

Story Background

In the writing workshop, you frequently give children responsibility for finding their own, personal writing topics. You may shy away from prompts or story starters because you have discovered that the writing is more skillful and children more motivated when they write about what they know. Much of their writing is personal, in the memoir genre. For example, Bob enjoys writing about birthdays—his brother's, his cousin's, and his own. Jeffrey has written a series of pieces about his trip to Disneyland. Some children like to write nonfiction about their interests. Laura frequently reads and writes about pandas. Many classrooms post a reference chart called "I Can Write About . . ." followed by a list: family, pets, vacations, friends, and so on. Children become accustomed to having choice about their topics, and some may think ahead of time about an upcoming writing period, at home, during soccer practice, or on the school playground. Every Monday morning for months the class has done the Weekend News assignment. Again, when there is a routine with a regular task or activity, you hope that children will be rehearsing for this job. Perhaps, with Weekend News, they will think about it during the weekend and decide on Saturday or Sunday what to write. The assignment helps children transition back into the school week with a regular, predictable writing activity. Children share weekend events with classmates while reading to partners at the end of the work period or listening in a circle to what others have written. Whatever the writing task, you have undoubtedly encountered a child as stymied as Cathy is on this morning. She may be unable to think of anything joyful or interesting to write about, or perhaps she is feeling stubborn or upset for some entirely different reason. She doesn't want or couldn't cope with my help. Nothing I say is any use to her. Cathy has several other jobs to do while Whitney teaches reading, but is only focused on her frustrating Weekend News.

Teaching Strategies

Can a child in Cathy's frame of mind be helped by an adult? There are times when you, the teacher, reach a barrier so high that you cannot be of service. On the other hand, I hoped and anticipated that Cathy was listening to my suggestions before I moved away to work with another child. Perhaps she could reconsider our conversation as she calmed down and began to realize that she would be held accountable for a carefully crafted Weekend News, one that met the standards that had been spelled out in this classroom.

Demonstrate Rehearsal

I have already mentioned the hope that students will think about writing their Weekend News ahead of time, during the weekend or on the school bus. If you want your students to do this, you can explicitly teach them about rehearsal. As you talk about this strategy, you can relate it to other rehearsals. Children who take dance or music lessons will immediately grasp the meaning of rehearsal because they are already doing it. The difference is that rehearsal for writing is mental work, while rehearsal for dance is physical. A think-aloud will help model this kind of planning for younger students. You can say, "Let's see. I need to write my weekly letter to my aunt. This is like Weekend News. What shall I tell her that is interesting? It can be about some small thing that happened, and I can write all the details. Yesterday my dog chewed the edge of the kitchen rug. I think he was upset because he was alone in the house for such a long time. I could write about that." And so on.

Minilessons about rehearsal help young children become aware of a strategy that is frequently used by writers. If you fail to bring it to their attention, they may never realize the possibilities of rehearsal or integrate it into their lives. Of course, one minilesson will not be enough; it will take several. I would suggest that you teach children about preparation and rehearsal at intervals rather than in one long series. Teach it perhaps twice, and later circle back and teach it again, and then again. Some students pick up a new concept the first time it is brought to their attention, while others are not ready to integrate it and need repeated encounters. It helps to vary the way you present the concept of rehearsal to accommodate different learning styles. You can use think-aloud, group conversation, an individual conference, or writing on a chart. Then review, including contributions by students on how they rehearse for different activities.

Introduce Guided Planning

Rehearsal can take the form of concrete and specific planning in class. One idea involves giving students a piece of scrap paper that is folded in quarters. Children number the boxes, right to left and top to bottom. They write in each box. Number one has a title or name: the topic. Box two has one sentence or phrase about the beginning of the piece. Box three contains information about the projected middle of the writing. Number four tells how the writer plans to conclude the piece: the ending. Moving from this bare-bones planning to writing takes guidance. Students need to learn how to think about filling in the spaces from box to box with details and elaboration for their written piece. Recently I saw a third-grade student take these boxes and simply rewrite what was in them, thinking he had done his job.

Remind at Dismissal Time

Another plan involves using the last few minutes of the school day to remind children about what they will be responsible for the next day. A few words from you, such as a reminder on Friday that they will be writing Weekend News on Monday and should think about it over the weekend, can reinforce rehearsal minilessons. If they can anticipate Monday morning, it helps them transition back to school. The same kind of reminder smoothes out other classroom activities, such as science investigations, math problem solving, and field trips. You will want to remind children to bring special materials to school or come dressed appropriately for an activity, such as a field day. Once you build reminders into your dismissal schedule you will think of many ways to use this technique.

Compose a Parent Newsletter

Another format for reminding children about Weekend News is to make sure parents know that this writing occurs every Monday morning. If you compose a Friday newsletter to parents to inform them about school activities, you can enlist their assistance for the events of the upcoming week. First you will want to explain Weekend News in detail. Then you can place a little box in your weekly newsletter for reminders. In this case, it might say, "Can you help your child think about what to write for Weekend News next Monday?" In this way, you ask parents to reinforce the concept of rehearsal. This strategy of using the newsletter will also be good for other school activities. For example, you could write, "Please remember to send the signed permission slip for our field trip to The Nature Center."

Create a Reference Chart

At the beginning of the year, support students by holding group discussions about what kinds of things they can write for Weekend News (or for birthday greetings, or whatever repeating assignment you plan to give). This puts all the ideas children have for writing topics in the public domain.

As well, create a chart that lists the children's ideas. Hang it in the room for reference so that all students can consult it when they reach a blind alley and feel they have nothing to write. You can refer children to the reference chart when you see they need help. There is power in this chart because it depersonalizes things a bit, and you are not in the position of making a suggestion and having it consistently refused, as Cathy did with me. The class can add to the chart whenever a new idea surfaces. Children enjoy attribution, so I would suggest that if John N. suggests writing about a grandparent visit for Weekend News, then place the word *grandparents* on the list followed by (J.N.), so everyone remembers it was his idea.

Generate a Personal List

Personal brainstorming may help a child like Cathy. In preparation for Weekend News, she could use a page in the back of her book to generate a list of weekend activities, adding the feelings she has about them: *Grocery store—don't like. Soccer—exciting.* Or, perhaps thinking about the weekend in a chronological fashion could help her recall the small things she did that might be sources for writing: *Pizza—yum. Letter from Grandma—yes!* Or she could think in categories, such as outdoor activities, food she ate, activities with siblings, and what her parents did. She can review this list on later Mondays when she is searching for topics.

Reread

There may be help for children within their own writing. Cathy could reread her previous entries in the Weekend News notebook. Often students find the kernel of a new writing idea in the writing they did weeks or even months ago. Rereading also gives them a bit of space in which to relax as they try to come up with something to write. Again, this is a strategy that can be taught to the whole class in minilessons. When students have backstop strategies they already know, they will require less adult intervention if they reach that moment of impasse.

Turn to a Partner

Another way to help children get started with an assignment is to ask them to discuss their plans with a partner. You may have engaged in this kind of activity in a teachers' workshop, so you know how useful it can be. Discussing plans or ideas with another person helps unlock your thoughts, just as getting feedback from another person is supportive. Listening to what your partner is planning may refresh your own ideas. You can ask students to turn to a partner and discuss their plans before they leave the morning circle. Children enjoy this activity. Once the work period is over, another step is for the class to hold a short discussion about how the partner work helped. This discussion will facilitate student understanding of partner power. Another option is to talk about whether or not they actually did what they planned with their partner. This leads to the realization that partner planning carries no firm obligation but is supportive as a way to begin.

Draw to Unlock Ideas

Ruth Hubbard (1989) writes, "Drawing is not just for children who can't yet write fluently, and creating pictures is not just part of rehearsal for writing. Images at any age are part of the serious business of making meaning—partners with words for communicating inner designs" (157). Frequently, when children cannot decide the details of what they want to write, drawing can help them unlock their thoughts. The booklets Whitney had for Weekend News, with space for a picture, were just right for this task. Young students like to draw first and think about the fine

134

"I just don't
*know what to
write."*

points of what they will write as they illustrate a projected piece. When I have worked with young children, someone will invariably ask, "Can I draw first?" The student who asks this question realizes intuitively that drawing is a strategy that assists in the discovery of what she wants to write.

Move On

When you reach that barrier you cannot surmount with a child like Cathy, then you know you need to move along and leave this writer to her own devices. She may be resisting your help for reasons you will never fathom. There are times when you cannot help no matter how hard you try. How do you decide when to back off? The line between being helpful and being a nuisance is delicate. Your gut feelings will tell you when to find an exit from a conference that is going nowhere. Sometimes a child is in a mood that will not permit her to accept suggestions from another person. When that happens, it is better to leave gracefully and spend your time working with someone else.

Conclusion

Your most important job is to help all children in your class. Every child is in a different place on the continuum in his skills and in his ability and willingness to accept help. Writing Weekend News is not the only time when you will discover students who are stymied as they try to fulfill their responsibilities. Your job is to teach long-term strategies as you show them how to access their thinking.

There are times when children are emotionally unable to fulfill an assignment such as writing Weekend News. Once in a while you will need to modify an assignment and give an altered task to a child who needs wiggle room. If you have a variety of strategies in your repertoire, you can assist a student who reaches that point where she is headed for a crash. You will want to help her avoid that collision and move ahead with her work. This will help her feel better about herself, about school, and about this particular assignment. Not long after I left Cathy, I hovered nearby to check on her. I found that she was busily at work on an illustration for her Weekend News. She had thought of a tiny family episode from Sunday morning's breakfast that she wanted to explore in her writing.

"Do I have to follow your directions?"

How to diversify instruction in the writing workshop.
- **Say yes to special requests**
- **Say no to special requests**
- **Diversify instruction**

Setting the Scene

School and community: Webster Elementary Magnet School, New Rochelle, New York, a small city in the New York metropolitan area

Teacher: Beth Eccleston

Description: Pull-out program for fifth graders identified for enrichment; I visited Beth's classroom eight times to do demonstration lessons in writing workshop as a staff developer for The Reading and Writing Project, and between lessons, students were writing almost daily as Beth propelled our work forward

The Story

With the children at my feet, I begin my demonstration of how to **explode the moment:**

> This afternoon we're going to focus on a strategy known as "explode the moment." When an author explodes the moment he takes a small event from his writing and adds both detail and emotion. Writing that is detailed and has feelings in it helps the reader create a vivid mental picture of what's happening. Another word for this is *elaboration*. When you explode the moment or elaborate, you create a piece of writing that packs a wallop. I'm going to show you what I mean through drafts of my own writing about my childhood dog, Rusty.

When my demonstration draws to a close, it is time for writers to do their work. These are my directions:

- Reread your notebook and find a piece of writing you really like.
- Locate some snippet of that writing where you think you can explode the moment.
- Practice and experiment with this strategy.

I remind students to elaborate with both detail and feeling. I suggest that they may find it helpful to talk it over quietly with a partner. I also ask if there is anything I need to clear up before they begin. Since there are no questions and students seem to understand the assignment, they leave the meeting area to begin work. However, Melanie lingers nearby and approaches me politely when everyone is gone. "Do I have to follow your directions?" she asks. "You see, I have a file cabinet of ideas in my head. I was hoping to work on one of the ideas today and begin something new."

Story Background

One of the firm foundations of the writing workshop is choice. You give children choice about topic selection and genre. They decide either to continue working on a piece or to begin something new. They decide when they want to revise and polish their writing. For a successful writing workshop, you must do the kind of teaching that gives children an awareness of possibility.

Young students in particular need to learn how to think about the possibilities within a topic. If they study a variety of genre, they can imagine writing a memoir, poetry, plays, or nonfiction. Studying story structure helps them envision a variety of ways to construct their pieces. A study of character development helps young writers to write about interesting people. A study of setting brings place to the forefront of their thinking. Your job is to teach a variety of minilessons, encourage them to do a lot of reading, and read aloud daily to increase the scope of their knowledge about literature. All these things help them envision the possibilities for writing.

Don Graves (1994) tells us, "When children choose their own topics, I can expect more of their writing. . . . I can focus my questions [in conference] on their initiative and their intentions" (107). Regie Routman (1991) notes, "Students and teachers must be free to choose their reading books and their writing topics most of the time. . . . Choice implies trust of students and teachers, and this trust does not come easily"

(18). Lucy Calkins ([1986] 1994) says, "Clearly, writing workshops need to be modeled after art studios and researchers' laboratories; we need to invite students to pursue their own important projects in an environment that is ongoing and stable and then move around among them—watching, demonstrating, and giving pointers" (15).

If you've taught writing workshop for any length of time, you are accustomed to providing your students with choice and expecting the kind of responsibility that accompanies it. But you know there are times when you may ask your class to try something new, and you anticipate that everyone in the class will experiment with the new strategy. After all, how will they know whether this idea will work for them as writers if they don't have the opportunity to try it out, perhaps several times? You may teach children to replace mundane words, such as *nice* and *stuff,* with an enriched vocabulary. You may introduce the use of rhetorical questions, alliteration, metaphor, or powerful leads. After a minilesson on any of these topics, you will probably ask your students to try the strategy.

Teaching Strategies

But what do you do if a child like Melanie comes to you and requests the opportunity to exercise her preferred choice instead? Should you say yes to her, or should you ask her to follow the directions you have given the rest of the class? The dilemma that she presented to me was similar to many decisions a teacher must make during the course of a day, a week, and a school year. A request may be about choice in reading materials, written assignments, homework, or social matters. Once you unleash the possibility of choice, children are eager to exercise it throughout the school day, and to take the responsibility that walks alongside it. Your job is to teach them how to make appropriate choices.

Say Yes to Special Requests

Giving Melanie permission to do what she had planned or rehearsed reinforces the everyday tenor and tenets of the writing workshop. Melanie was, as Donald Graves (1994) describes, "a child in a constant state of composition" (107). I had known her for three years as I worked in this school, and I enjoyed watching her grow as a writer. She was a conscientious person, a real writer, who had demonstrated her interest and skill in craft.

A filing cabinet in her head! What a delightful way to express the fact that she was doing exactly what we hope our writing students will begin to do—immerse themselves in that "constant state of composition." She knew that she was going to write in Beth's class four or five afternoons a week, and she had obviously spent time away from class anticipating her choices. Today she was standing ready to pull open one drawer of her filing cabinet, reach into it, and begin a new piece of writing she had already been composing in her mind. She was disappointed to think she might have to put her plans on hold.

You may have a different opinion, but I did not want to deny her the opportunity to follow through with her own ideas. I wanted to encourage her to keep that cabinet filled with its drawers ready to be pulled open. So, rather than tell her she must focus on the strategy with the rest of the class at that time, I asked her to take a careful look at the first draft of this new piece and spend time later to practice exploding the moment with part of that writing. I suggested that she do this at home, and I told her that I would appreciate seeing it the following week when I returned.

I deeply respect the way she approached me. She was quiet and did it when the other students were already occupied with their own concerns as they began to follow the directions I had given. Before I left for the day I explained to Beth what had happened. She could help to hold Melanie accountable, if that was necessary, though I very much doubted that any teacher intervention would be needed.

Say No to Special Requests

Perhaps in my early years of teaching I would have been inclined to say no to special requests. I interpreted consistency in a more literal way. I still do feel strongly about consistency, but I view it differently now. In those years I may have had difficulty realizing how to make an exception for Melanie and to diversify instruction.

Years ago I would have asked her to put aside the idea from her filing cabinet and follow the directions given to the class. I could have explained my reasons for asking her to comply, and she, no doubt, would have accepted them. Then there would have been no danger that another student in the room would also want some kind of relaxation to the assignment. If you are worried about such a eruption, then you won't feel comfortable saying yes to a student like Melanie. You would be perfectly justified denying her request.

Diversify Instruction

One way to keep students motivated and productive is by diversifying instruction within your classroom. When you have a serious, conscientious student like Melanie, you can easily give her some latitude in responding to an assignment that is designed to help her learn a new writing strategy. You don't want to set up a situation where she will avoid or not experiment with the strategy you have just taught, because you know it is an important idea for writers to consider. But you don't want her to think she is so tightly confined that you are standing in the way of her personal plans and pace for writing.

I tried to work around the issue by asking her to experiment with exploding the moment at home. I gave her a deadline. I honored her request because I knew Melanie and felt sure that she would follow through promptly and appropriately to fulfill her responsibilities. Did she do it? Of course she did, and she wrote with her usual panache and enjoyment. She appreciated the flexibility and responded to the challenge.

Another way to offer choice and diversify instruction is to lay out several strategies for practice: explode the moment, replace mundane words, and create a lead that will draw in the reader. Select strategies that have already been taught in separate minilessons over a period of time. Then you can have sign-up sheets for your record keeping and for student accountability, as students sign a list to show which strategy they will practice on a given day or set of days. A glance at the sign-up sheets will tell you what you need to encourage each child to do to diversify his practice. If you organize the class this way, a group of simultaneous share sessions, prearranged by strategy, can wrap up the writing session as students teach each other with demonstrations of their work.

Conclusion

You know that you do any job better when you are committed to the task or assignment. Compare how you feel about arranging a beautiful bouquet of flowers to washing the kitchen floor. If your administrator asks you to teach reading groups using textbooks and scripted lessons when you believe in using literature with student choice and more individualized instruction, it is difficult for you to follow the administrator's directive. There is a difference in how you feel about performing a task because you *have* to do it as compared to doing that same job because you *want* to do it.

Transfer these statements to a student's compliance with directions given by the teacher. Do you want to be unbending when a student requests a waiver? Personally, I don't, but that is my style, the way I prefer to run a classroom. The purpose of this story is to open a door for you to think about the assignments you give in fresh and flexible ways. Giving students choice does not mean you are being so permissive that they are only doing what they want to do. As you become accustomed to teach reading and writing workshops, you will learn that it is possible to listen to children and follow their lead at times that are appropriate. As Skolnick (2000) explains, "Choice enlivens our existence and grants us the chance to make decisions and try new things. Choice with responsibility is the backbone of our democracy. It must have its tender roots in the classrooms of young learners" (112–113).

When a student like Melanie presents you with an alternative, your job is to slow down and carefully consider the implications of her request. What you decide to do will be up to you. I have attempted to demonstrate that there isn't one answer to her question. As you follow your own guiding lights, the children in your classroom who are like Melanie will be satisfied with your answer. Be consistent with yourself and the way you lay the path through both steep and level ground for the students in your care.

"I thought I should put one in every time I wrote an *s* at the end of a word."

How to teach punctuation and other skills.

- **Construct reference charts**
- **Examine reading materials**
- **Demonstrate**
- **Focus through individual or small-group teaching**

Setting the Scene

School and community: Coleytown Elementary School, Westport, Connecticut, a suburban district
Teacher: Julianne Dow
Description: Third-grade, self-contained class; Julianne is an experienced teacher, but because she was new to the Westport staff, I was her mentor and visited regularly for writing workshop

The Story

This is a story about mechanics, not about craft. You know it is important for students to learn the conventions of written English. These rules are sometimes a bit obscure for youngsters since there are so many inconsistencies and irregularities. This being said, you expect all students to put effort into written work and do their best. Students need to learn to automatically spell as correctly as they can, to capitalize, and to put in punctuation. They also need to learn about apostrophes and hyphenation.

It is time for my weekly visit to Julianne Dow's class. The third graders are engaged in a memoir study. The minilesson is complete, and children set to work as they continue to draft entries in their notebooks. Sometimes Julianne shadows me, but today we plan to **work the room** separately, conferring with individual writers. We each carry a clipboard with a record-keeping sheet (see Figure 4 on page 9). Julianne looks over her record for the week and suggests I begin with Kayla and Artie today.

141

I sit down next to Kayla. I ask how it's going. Earlier in the week Julianne introduced the pattern used by Jamie Lee Curtis (1993) in *When I Was Little: A Four-Year-Old's Memoir of Her Youth*. Kayla is experimenting with this pattern, writing an amusing entry about how food spilled off her plate and fell on her cat when she was little, and she has drawn a detailed, colorful picture of her cat covered with spaghetti sauce. She has written, "But now the food alway's stay's on my plate." When I ask about the apostrophes, she replies, "I thought I should put one in every time I wrote an *s* at the end of a word."

I teach her a brief lesson about when the apostrophe is supposed to be used. She practices a few examples, which I dictate to her, and we discuss them further. I know that her understanding is probably rudimentary, but this is enough for today, so I move along to Artie. He is writing about his first love—basketball—using the same pattern from Jamie Lee Curtis. He says that his father used to have to lift him up so he could drop the ball in the basket, but now that he is bigger, when he shoots by himself "the ball often goe's in the hoop." A third child, Amy, has put an apostrophe *s* after each name, such as "Amy's wanted to go out and play." When she reads it aloud she looks puzzled because she knows it doesn't make sense. I ask her why she put the apostrophe there, and she replies, "Because a name is there."

I am sure that if I had found time to confer with more students that afternoon I would have turned up other instances where writers had misused the apostrophe and had their own unique reasons for doing so. This story could be written about almost any second- or third-grade classroom I've ever seen because the overgeneralization about apostrophe usage is one of the most common things you can see in young writers. When I was teaching second grade, many children used one every time an *s* was added to a word, even to make a plural, such as in *two cats*. Once boys and girls become aware of the apostrophe in their reading or are introduced to some basic rules by a teacher they use it relentlessly, assuming that they are doing the right thing.

Story Background

Students often misunderstand how to write plurals, possessives, and contractions. An amusing article by Sarah Lyall (2001) in the *New York Times* describes a grammarian in Boston, England, who is taking his town to task for misplaced or missing apostrophes in signs. He has formed the Apostrophe Protection Society and delivers letters to local businesses whose signs are not correctly written. Lyall notes, "The correspondence spurred by his apostrophe campaign has reminded him that there is a big, imprecise world out there, with many outstanding grammar and punctuation problems" (A4).

And no wonder. I looked up the definition of *possessive* in our *Webster's New International Dictionary* (1960) only to find a very long and rather confusing entry: "The possessive case, a word in that case, or an equivalent case phrase, as with *of.*" It goes on to state, "Present usage favors the following treatment of the apostrophe in forming possessives: (1) Nouns not ending in a sibilant sound, whether singular or plural, add *'s,* (*dog's, man's, men's*). (2) Singular nouns ending in an *s-* or *z-* sound, when of one syllable, add *'s* (*James's; Mars's; Hicks's*); when two or more syllables taking accent on the last, add *'s* if the last syllable is not preceded by an *s-* or *z-*sound (*Thomas's; Andrews's*); but when the last syllable is preceded by an *s-* or *z-* sound, they add simply the apostrophe (*Moses'; princess';*) . . ." Note the words "present usage," which implies the possibility of change. I have not even mentioned contractions. After reading the dictionary I thought, "Even I am somewhat confused." But if children are developmentally ready, they can certainly learn the difference between plurals and possessives if they are taught a series of lessons over time.

In the same way, children overuse hyphenation and do it incorrectly. Recently in Stephanie Schock's second-grade classroom at Coleytown Elementary School, where I was acting as Stephanie's mentor, it seemed necessary to teach a minilesson about hyphenation. I had noticed that children were splitting words incorrectly when they ran out of room instead of writing the entire word on the next line. When I asked the class why one would hyphenate a word, Carl put forth a very interesting theory. He thought that if you had an even number of letters in a word, his example being ten, you would put five on one line and five on the next. I think young children like to try out new ideas, like apostrophes and hyphenation, when they first notice them, before they realize there are rules. They may develop theories that seem logical to them, as Carl did. Our job is to help them integrate the rules that have been developed.

Teaching Strategies

Almost everyone in a class of seven-, eight-, or even nine-year-olds would benefit from instruction on the use of apostrophes, as you can readily see when you look closely at their written work. It requires considerable exposure and practice to help children approximate the correct usage of apostrophes. You will want to combine minilessons with individualized

144

*"I thought I
should put one in
every time I
wrote an s at the
end of a word."*

teaching to work on this skill. When you monitor written work carefully, you can help young students outgrow their natural tendency to add the *'s* whenever they think they see an opportunity. I know grown-ups who write the word *it's* incorrectly. They use the contraction *it's* when they are writing the possessive *its food*, meaning the cat's food. It's (!) confusing because, as you can see, this is an example of a possessive where you don't add an apostrophe.

Construct Reference Charts

Reference charts that help your students learn to use apostrophes can grow from the minilessons you teach and from examples that present themselves during the school day. They should be constructed in the context of reading and writing or they will be meaningless. These charts cannot simply be a list of words with apostrophes. For example, they need to contain phrases of two or more words, so students can learn conventions such as the distinction between the use of *its* (a possessive) and *it's* (a contraction). If, in the days and weeks following a series of minilessons, you see a misuse of the apostrophe, you can talk individually with the writer. Then, later, with the writer's permission, you can bring that example to the attention of the whole class and add it to the reference chart. Of course, reference charts are never complete. You can add to them at any time that seems appropriate for the teaching and learning that is taking place in the classroom.

Examine Reading Materials

You can help students understand the proper use of apostrophes when you ask them to examine the books they are reading to see what is done in them. Children can pop sticky notes into a book or jot down the phrases with apostrophes as they read. These examples can be discussed later so they don't interrupt the flow of reading. This might be a good time to tell your students that every published writer has a copy editor who has the job of making sure that the text is as perfect as it can be before it is actually put in print. They will be interested to learn that the copy editor needs to be skilled in all uses of our language, including spelling, punctuation, grammar, and other conventions.

If your class subscribes to a student newspaper, such as *Time for Kids* or *Scholastic News*, or has a collection of *Ranger Rick* magazines, these are other sources to help students notice written conventions. Children can use highlighters or markers if they notice a plural or possessive when reading a student newspaper. I recommend that you discuss these details separately from the content of the paper. In other words, you will not wish to interrupt the reading comprehension but will talk about the mechanics in a different discussion. Later, when students take their copy of the paper home, if highlighters have been used, their parents will become aware of what you are doing in class and will be able to help you teach and monitor the use of these conventions in homework assignments, letter writing, and other writing tasks the children perform at home.

Demonstrate
Modeling is yet another strategy that will help students learn to distinguish between plurals and possessives. When you write on chart paper to demonstrate for the class, you may want to use the think-aloud technique. You can say, "Let's see, how do I write *its* here? Am I saying the words it is (*it's*) or am I saying the bowl belongs to my dog—*its* bowl?" As you make your thinking available for students, you help them learn to go through a similar, thoughtful process as they compose. It is important to point out that you are doing a think-aloud so they can begin to think in the same way.

Focus Through Individual or Small-Group Teaching
Many children can get this problem under their belt fairly easily once it is consistently called to their attention. By the time they finish third grade or fourth grade, most students will be using apostrophes correctly. For the few who cannot, additional gentle coaching, either individually or in small groups, will be required. It is important to focus on how many times a child uses the possessive, contraction, or plural correctly as opposed to how many mistakes there are. A positive spin is crucial for both students and parents, who may tend to focus on errors rather than successes.

Can we expect 100-percent learning on this subject? Of course not. It is like any literacy learning. There will be a wide range of development and accomplishment in your class. Some children will not be ready or able to learn this until they are older—in fourth or fifth or even sixth grade. As the article in the *New York Times* reveals, some adults even misuse the apostrophe. Your job is to do the best you can, and expect the most of everyone. You can be guided by the assumption that children will attempt to live up to your expectations if they possibly can.

Conclusion

The use of apostrophes is linked to spelling. In her foreword to *Spelling in Use*, Sandra Wilde (1996) says, "An informed, attentive teacher can create a powerful, effective curriculum in which spelling grows out of children's own explorations with spelling as they write" (x). The same is true for learning to use apostrophes correctly. No one has ever claimed that becoming literate in English and being highly skilled in written English is easy. I think of the ads I occasionally hear on the radio for tapes that are intended to help adults increase their vocabulary and thus make them sound more impressive to others. Writing literate English easily and with accuracy is even more daunting than using spoken language.

Certain conventions are used to judge speakers and writers. The conventions surrounding written work, such as vocabulary, capitals, periods, quotation marks, apostrophes, hyphenation, and paragraphing are among the things your students need to master. They can integrate these conventions when they are taught and consistently reinforced in context at an appropriate developmental level.

Here is a story from a second-grade class I taught. One of my pet peeves is the all too common usage "me and my friend . . ." One day I decided to tackle this, even though I knew that perhaps I was tilting at windmills. I gave a short talk explaining that many people spoke and wrote this way, but it was incorrect. I stated that the proper usage was "my friend and I" and gave children some short examples of how they could figure out when to use the word *me* and when to use *I*.

For the balance of the year, Bill, a bright and testy student, went out of his way to write "me and my brother," or "me and John." Then he would underline those words at least five times, as boldly as he could. He made sure that everyone around him saw what he had done, and he called attention to it whenever he shared in the group. I knew that Bill had really integrated what I said and that he would always remember it. My teaching was not in vain, in spite of his carefully orchestrated bit of defiance.

Thinking about this story convinces me again that it is important to make the effort to help children with the nuances and fine points of spoken and written language even when the distinctions seem difficult for some of them to grasp. This is part of the sacred charge you accepted when you decided to become a teacher: to educate all students to the best of their abilities, in the most conscientious way you can.

Afterword

Connections. Connections. You probably know the song that goes "the hip bone is connected to the leg bone, the leg bone is connected to the ankle bone," and so on. As I think back about what's written here, it seems to me that everything is connected. This is true for the people in your teaching and learning life and it holds for the things associated with teaching and learning. Let me explain what I mean.

You, the teacher, are connected to each learner in your classroom. An essential way to improve that connection is to listen to children. Youngsters can help guide you hour by hour and day by day. What children say and do can be the springboard for your every move in the classroom. For example, if a child asks if he can write some things that are not totally true in a memoir piece, I realize I need to teach all my students to understand how authors blur the line between fact and fiction. This is but one case of how and why a teacher needs to stay firmly connected to her students. There are many other examples inside these covers.

Your students are, in turn, connected to you. As we look at young children, the connections are more obvious, almost like an umbilical cord. When students mature, it is natural for them to loosen the cord, but the ties still need to be strong. Students are more available to learn and grow, to assimilate the skills and concepts you teach, when they are connected to you. If a student is not linked, then you should be concerned, because that student may be unable to learn. She may be in her own bubble, unconnected to you or her classmates.

Students are connected to each other. They learn a great deal from each other, for better or for worse. They constantly monitor each other's behavior and talk. This makes it important for you to model and coach continually and consistently. You want them to copy the behavior of positive leaders, not negative ones. After several months, if you and everyone else has done a constructive job, if pleasure and joy are part of the classroom as well as hard work, the entire community should come together to act as a beneficial influence on each member and any new member who comes to join the group.

You and your students are connected to the curriculum that you teach and that they are expected to learn. You want to be intimately familiar with the concepts and skills in that curriculum so your teaching can become an act that leaves energy for you to be a flexible, accurate observer and listener in the classroom. Your students will be connected to the curriculum and motivated to learn if you present it in appropriate and enjoyable ways. You can help them achieve that connection if you teach deliberately and use the curriculum as a platform for serious purpose, together with humor and play.

There are additional connections to the objects in your classroom: the books, the reference charts you create, the math manipulatives—the tools with which you and your students work. These things support learning, so it is important that you are thoughtful about what you introduce to sustain your teaching. As I visit different rooms, I see a difference between organization and purpose, on the one hand, and clutter and chaos on the other. Every couple of weeks you might think of being an interior decorator, to look at the space and decide what things distract attention from the central messages. If you and your students are not connected to the things in the room, they serve no purpose and should be put or thrown away. For example, if children are not using the environmental print you have placed on the walls or hung on lines, then there is no purpose in having it there. You either need to teach them to use that print or take it down.

When all these connections are tied together, they become an important gift. Your students will be active learners who respect each other and share their thinking with you and their peers. You will be ready to listen and learn from them, which is the point: listening to children so they can guide you toward more relevant, appropriate teaching. These children are your partners, and together you can walk toward common goals.

Glossary

Book basket   A container holding books that are classified by author, subject, or reading level. Organizing books in baskets helps children locate the titles they are seeking, especially in a classroom where there are many books. Books can be organized in baskets by the teacher or by the class. A title for the basket is placed in a prominent place on the front of each basket to make the search easier. A classroom library may contain both baskets and shelves with books organized differently. Of course, these baskets need to be reorganized with some degree of frequency because the books do get mixed up.

Choice   A term used in workshop teaching. Students, not teachers, choose the books they wish to read or their topics for writing. Students also choose whether to continue reading or to abandon books, and to work longer on a piece of writing or to begin something new. Responsibility for this type of decision is placed on the student. The teacher gives guidance for exercising reasonable choices and responsibilities by modeling and coaching.

Explode the moment   A writing strategy designed to take a section of writing and embroider it with detail and emotion. The purpose is to pull readers into the piece of writing by helping them understand the feelings and details of what occurred in the story. Another word for this is *elaboration*.

Fishbowl activity   A teaching activity in which a teacher and another person discuss, while students listen, a topic that is germane to the work in the class. For example, two teachers can discuss their strategies for choosing books or looking for a writing topic. After the brief adult discussion is over, the teacher can delve into it in more detail in a minilesson, if needed.

Kidwatching   The act of closely observing students. This observation may take place in the classroom, while moving from class to class, during recess, or at any appropriate time of day. The purpose is to inform the teacher so that instruction may be modified to fit the needs and interests of the class, to aid in parent communications, to share information with other teachers who work with the child, and so forth. Teachers usually have a form or forms that they use to record relevant observations.

Meeting area   A clearly defined area in the classroom where students can gather together for discussions, choral reading, and other group activities. Children are instructed ahead of time to sit in a cluster or a circle. Teachers use both, depending on the activity. Some teachers mark the floor or rug with tape to indicate exactly where children are expected to sit.

Minilesson   A short focused moment of direct teaching, usually at the beginning of a reading, writing, math, social studies, or science class. The lesson is designed to set the stage for the practice students will be doing. It lasts approximately ten minutes, no longer. Examples of minilessons are:

- Read or refer to a previously read piece of literature for a specific purpose, such as focusing on the way an author uses language or develops the story structure.
- Introduce a new strategy for reading response, such as talking or writing about the character.
- Teach how to play a math game.
- Focus on how to have a peer writing conference. Role-play may be included.

Read the room   An activity designed to help a writer find an appropriate writing topic. The student looks in detail at everything in the room and associates ideas with items, such as a reference chart with descriptive words on it, a science project, the alphabet chart. For example, if the science project involves peat pots with seeds planted by students, perhaps the writer will be reminded about working in the garden at home and decide to write about that.

Reference chart   A chart constructed in class by the teacher and students. It hangs in the classroom to help students with their work.

The language on the chart is that of students. The chart may be a set of classroom rules, a list of topics for writing, or a list of suggestions for how to conduct group work. The chart is always in progress; it is never complete, and the class can always amend or add to it. It is specific to one group or class, and is never made ahead of time by the teacher or used from year to year.

Rehearsal   A term used in the writing workshop. It is the thinking writers devote to planning a piece of writing before they begin to write. For example, during the weekend students may engage in rehearsal for writing their Weekend News, so they come to school with their ideas ready. They know that they will be engaged in this writing at a certain time, on a particular day, and so they rehearse for that writing. Rehearsal may also be applied to reading. A student may rehearse, to himself, plans for book club talk or a reader's response.

Seed idea   A kernel or theme that appears frequently in a child's first-draft writing. This theme may later be developed into a more finished piece of writing. For example, if a student frequently writes about her brother, she may wish to write a new piece about her brother, work on it, revise it, and polish it into a finished piece of writing.

SSR or Sustained Silent Reading   A block of time in the daily schedule for independent reading. The book is chosen by the student. Generally, teachers do not permit talking or walking around during this time. The teacher may be reading as a role model, but more often he will be working quietly with an individual student. The length of time for SSR depends upon the age of the children. Reading time is usually increased as children become more accustomed to this activity. It is designed to practice reading skills. This is sometimes called DEAR time, or Drop Everything And Read.

Think-aloud   The teacher makes her thinking public for students. For example, she verbalizes what she predicts the author is going to write to solve a mystery or a problem in a book. The teacher may think aloud about the way she writes. By doing this, the teacher demonstrates two things: how to engage in a particular strategy, and why that strategy is helpful to a reader or writer. This negates what is called "assumptive teaching"—teaching that assumes students understand the terminology we use and the reasons we ask them to do things, when it's possible they do not.

Touchstone book   A well-loved, admired picture or chapter book that a teacher or student uses over and over again to examine the craft of writing. A student writer may wish to emulate and use the same writing techniques in her own writing. The teacher may use a touchstone text repeatedly for minilessons and conferences to help children learn about craft.

Wait time   The teacher paces his verbal responses carefully, waiting to make certain a student is finished speaking or gathering her thoughts. Wait time is important when a student is answering a question. It gives the student an opportunity to think through and say all she wishes to at a particular time. Students are taught to use wait time, as well.

Work the room   The act of teaching while students are working individually or in groups. The teacher circulates through the classroom, making observations and recording them. She may talk with individuals or to small groups. The purpose is more focused, individualized teaching, but since children may be listening to the transactions with other students, broader teaching is often being accomplished.

Bibliography

Anderson, Carl. 2000. *How's It Going?* Portsmouth, NH: Heinemann.

Atwell, Nancie. 1998. *In the Middle: New Understandings About Writing, Reading, and Learning.* Portsmouth, NH: Heinemann.

Brazelton, T. Berry, M.D., and Stanley I. Greenspan, M.D. 2000. *The Irreducible Needs of Children.* Cambridge, MA: Perseus.

Brown, Margaret Wise. 1947. *Goodnight Moon.* New York: Harper.

Bunting, Eve. 1989. *The Wednesday Surprise.* New York: Clarion.

Calkins, Lucy McCormick. 2001. *The Art of Teaching Reading.* New York: Addison-Wesley.

———. [1986] 1994. *The Art of Teaching Writing.* Portsmouth, NH: Heinemann.

Corbalis, Judy. 1989. *The Ice Cream Heroes.* Boston: Little, Brown.

Curtis, Jamie Lee. 1993. *When I Was Little: A Four-Year-Old's Memoir of Her Youth.* New York: HarperCollins.

Dexter, Catherine. 1985. *The Oracle Doll.* New York: Four Winds Press.

Dunning, Stephen, Edward Lueders, and Hugh Smith, eds. 1967. *Reflections on a Gift of Watermelon Pickle . . . And Other Modern Verse.* New York: Lothrop, Lee & Shepard.

Ernst, Karen. 1994. *Picturing Learning: Artists and Writers in the Classroom.* Portsmouth, NH: Heinemann.

Fletcher, Ralph, and JoAnn Portalupi. 1998. *Craft Lessons: Teaching Writing K–8.* York, ME: Stenhouse.

Fox, Mem. 2001. *Reading Magic, Why Reading Aloud to Our Children Will Change Their Lives Forever.* San Diego: Harcourt Brace.

————. 1985. *Wilfred Gordon McDonald Partridge*. Brooklyn, NY and La Jolla, CA: Kane/Miller.

Fraser, Jane. 1998. *Teacher to Teacher: A Guidebook for Effective Mentoring*. Portsmouth, NH: Heinemann.

———— and Donna Skolnick. 1994. *On Their Way: Celebrating Second Graders as They Read and Write*. Portsmouth, NH: Heinemann.

Goodman, Kenneth S., Yetta M. Goodman, and Wendy Hood, eds. 1989. *The Whole Language Evaluation Book*. Portsmouth, NH: Heinemann.

Graves, Donald H. 2001. Inservice Talk to Staff. May 15. Westport, CT.

————. 1994. *A Fresh Look at Writing*. Portsmouth, NH: Heinemann.

————. 1992. *Explore Poetry*. Portsmouth, NH: Heinemann.

Gwynne, Fred. 1976. *A Chocolate Moose for Dinner*. New York: Prentice Hall.

————. 1970. *The King Who Rained*. New York: Prentice Hall.

Heard, Georgia. 1999. *Awakening the Heart: Exploring Poetry in Elementary and Middle School*. Portsmouth, NH: Heinemann.

Hindley, Joanne. 1996. *In the Company of Children*. York, ME: Stenhouse.

Hopping, Jean. 1995. *Hurricanes*. New York: Scholastic.

Hubbard, Ruth. 1989. *Authors of Pictures, Draughtsmen of Words*. Portsmouth, NH: Heinemann.

Kozol, Jonathan. 1995. *Amazing Grace: The Lives of Children and the Conscience of a Nation*. New York: Crown.

Laminack, Lester L., and Katie Wood. 1996. *Spelling in Use: Looking Closely at Spelling in Whole Language Classrooms*. Urbana, IL: National Council of Teachers of English.

Leach, Penelope. 1994. *Children First: What Our Society Must Do— And Is Not Doing—For Our Children Today*. New York: Knopf.

Levine, Arthur. 2000. "Tomorrow's Education, Made to Measure." *The New York Times*, December 22, A-33.

Lienhard, John. 2000. "Engines of Our Ingenuity." *Morning Edition*. National Public Radio, Program 626, August 23.

Lisle, Janet Taylor. 1993. *Forest*. New York: Scholastic.

Lyall, Sarah. 2001. "Minder of Misplaced Apostrophes Scolds a Town." 2001. *New York Times*, June 16. A4.

Martin, Bill Jr., and John Archambault. 1989. *Chicka Chicka Boom Boom*. New York: Simon & Schuster.

Mathews, Jay. 2001. "Education's Different Drummer." *The Washington Post*, January 9, A-10.

Merriam, Eve. 1967. "How to eat a poem." *In Reflections on a Gift of Watermelon Pickle . . . And Other Modern Verse,* eds. Stephen Dunning, Edward Lueders, and Hugh Smith. New York: Lothrop, Lee & Shepard.

Nelson, Jane. 1987. *Positive Discipline.* New York: Ballantine.

Paley, Vivian Gussin. 1992. *You Can't Say You Can't Play.* Cambridge, MA and London, UK: Harvard University Press.

Peterson, Ralph. 1992. *Life in a Crowded Place: Making a Learning Community.* Portsmouth, NH: Heinemann.

Peterson, Ralph, and Mary Ann Eeds. 1990. *Grand Conversations: Literature Groups in Action.* New York: Scholastic.

Porter, Carol. 1990. "Student Created Units: Choice Collaboration and Connections." In *Talking About Books: Creating Literate Communities,* eds. Kathy Gnagey Short and Kathryn Mitchell Pierce. Portsmouth, NH: Heinemann.

Ray, Katie Wood. 1999. *Wondrous Words: Writers and Writing in the Elementary Classroom.* Urbana, IL: National Council Teachers of English.

Routman, Regie. 1991. *Invitations: Changing as Teachers and Learners K–12.* Toronto, Canada: Irwin Publishing; Portsmouth, NH: Heinemann.

Rylant, Cynthia. 1998. *The Bird House.* New York: Blue Sky Press.

———. 1985. *The Relatives Came.* New York: Bradbury Press.

Say, Allen. 1993. *Grandfather's Journey.* Boston: Houghton Mifflin.

Schmeltz, Susan Alton. 1983. "Paper Dragons." In *The Random House Book of Poetry for Children,* ed. Jack Prelutsky. New York: Random House.

Skolnick, Donna. 2000. *More than Meets the Eye.* Portsmouth, NH: Heinemann.

Smith, Frank. 1985. *Reading Without Nonsense.* 2d Ed. New York: Teachers College Press.

Trelease, Jim. 1984. *The Read-Aloud Handbook.* New York: Penguin.

Warner, Gertrude Chandler. 1977. *The Boxcar Children.* Morton Grove, IL: Albert Whitman.

Watson, Dorothy J. 1990. "Show Me: Whole Language Evaluation of Literature Groups." In *Talking About Books: Creating Literate Communities,* eds. Kathy Gnagey Short and Kathryn Mitchell Pierce. Portsmouth, NH: Heinemann.

Webster's New International Dictionary of the English Language: Second Edition. 1960. Springfield, MA: G. and C. Merriam.

Webster's Ninth New Collegiate Dictionary. 1983. Springfield, MA: Merriam & Webster.

Wilde, Sandra. 1996. Foreword *Spelling in Use.* Lester Laminack and Katie Wood. Champaign, IL: NCTE.

Wood, Chip. 1999. *Time to Teach, Time to Learn: Changing the Pace of School.* Greenfield, MA: The Northeast Foundation for Children.

Yolen, Jane. 1997. *Miz Berlin Walks.* New York: Philomel.

———. 1996. *Welcome to the Sea of Sand.* New York: Putnam's.

Index